Issue 4 December 1998

Methodology

Special Issue

Edited by Anthea Jarvis

Edited by Dr. Valerie Steele

Fashion Theory

The Journal of Dress, Body & Culture

BERG

Fashion Theory: The Journal of Dress, Body & Culture

Editor
Dr. Valerie Steele
The Museum at the Fashion Institute of Technology, E201
Seventh Avenue at 27th Street
New York, NY 10001-5992
USA
Fax: +1 212 924 3958
e-mail: steelemajor@earthlink.net

Aims and Scope
The importance of studying the body as a site for the deployment of discourses is well-established in a number of disciplines. By contrast, the study of fashion has, until recently, suffered from a lack of critical analysis. Increasingly, however, scholars have recognized the cultural significance of self-fashioning, including not only clothing but also such body alterations as tattooing and piercing. *Fashion Theory* takes as its starting point a definition of 'fashion' as the cultural construction of the embodied identity. It aims to provide an interdisciplinary forum for the rigorous analysis of cultural phenomena ranging from footbinding to fashion advertising.

Anyone wishing to submit an article, interview, or a book, film or exhibition review for possible publication in this journal should contact Valerie Steele (at the address listed below) or the Editorial Department at Berg (150 Cowley Road, Oxford, OX4 1JJ, UK; e-mail: enquiry@berg.demon.co.uk).

Notes for Contributors can be found at the back of the journal.

ISSN: 1362-704X

Ordering Information	Four issues per volume.	One volume per annum.	1998: Volume 2
By mail:	Berg Publishers, 150 Cowley Road, Oxford, OX4 1JJ, UK.		
By fax:	+44 (0) 1865 791165		
By telephone:	+44 (0) 1865 245104		
By e-mail:	enquiry@berg.demon.co.uk		
Inquiries	Editorial: Kathryn Earle, Managing Editor. e-mail: kearle@berg1.demon.co.uk		
	Production: Sara Everett. e-mail: severett@berg.demon.co.uk		
	Advertising + subscriptions: Paul Millicheap. e-mail: pmillicheap@berg.demon.co.uk		
Subscription Rates:	Institutional base list subscription price: £86.00, US$120.00.	Individuals' subscription price: £35.00, US$48.00.	
Reprints of Individual Articles	Copies of individual articles may be obtained from the Publishers at the appropriate fees. Write to: Berg, 150 Cowley Road, Oxford, OX4 1JJ, UK.	Printed in the United Kingdom. DECEMBER 1998	

Contents

Editor
Dr. Valerie Steele
The Museum at the Fashion
    Institute of Technology, E201
Seventh Avenue at 27th Street
New York, NY 10001-5992
USA

Fax +1 212 924 3958
e-mail: steelemajor@earthlink.net

BERG

BERG

Fashion Theory, Volume 2, Issue 4, pp.299–300
Reprints available directly from the Publishers.
Photocopying permitted by licence only.

Platt Hall

Letter from the Editor

Anthea Jarvis

Anthea Jarvis is the Keeper of Costume at the Gallery of Costume, Manchester.

In July 1997 the Gallery of Costume, Platt Hall, Manchester, England, celebrated its 50th anniversary. It had opened in July 1947 to house and display the exceptionally large and fine collection of women's dress collected since 1930 by Drs. C. Willett and Phillis Cunnington and recently purchased by Manchester Corporation. As well as collecting dress, the Cunningtons researched and wrote on dress history, so it seemed appropriate to celebrate the Gallery's half-century with a conference that took as its theme the history of dress and fashion studies, and the various and very diverse approaches to this subject taken today. Taking as its title *Dress in History: Studies and Approaches*, the conference took place in Manchester in early July 1997.

The history of dress and fashion was not studied seriously in academic circles before the 1960s. Previously the books of the small number of dress historians, notably C. Willett and Phillis Cunnington, James Laver and Doris Langley Moore, who based their work on surviving historic dress in their own or public collections, and on contemporary prints, paintings and fashion plates, were read chiefly by museum curators, teachers, and theatrical designers. The first academics to research the history of dress were art historians, followed by economic historians, who had for some time previously studied textile manufacture, consumption, marketing and distribution. By the 1970s various other disciplines were staking a claim; design history, gender studies and cultural and media studies. These new academic approaches to dress study tended to prioritize social and political contexts over the older concerns of museum researchers to describe and analyze the garments themselves. As shown in Lou Taylor's article in this issue, in some academic circles it was fashionable to pour scorn on such 'hemline histories' and their alleged concern with the significance of every hook and frill. Dress history was not in fact the only historical study area to undergo this transition; there were similar developments in maritime and military history, among others. One of the themes that the conference aimed to address was the current divergence between object-based study, carried out by museum curators and makers of reproduction dress, and university studies of dress and fashion, usually based on written sources, images and statistics, but rarely on the real thing. The former, today's Cunningtons, Lavers and Langley-Moores, often feel dress study has been appropriated by the theorists, and buried in complex and inaccessible language.

The twenty seven papers given at the conference covered five approaches to dress study: object-based, art history, economic history, cultural history and reproduction dress for theater and re-enactment use. That such a wide range of approaches was presented and discussed contributed greatly to the conference's success. I am delighted that it is possible to publish six of the papers in this special volume of *Fashion Theory*. Further papers will appear in *Costume 32* to be published in June 1999.

Dress history as a subject is seen in a totally different light by the students of the 1990s, who have been brought up with the concepts of postmodernism and poststructuralism. The language and methodologies of fifty years ago are no longer adequate structures for modern approaches. Our fiftieth Anniversary Conference at Platt Hall demonstrated how far the parameters of dress history and its sister disciplines have broadened since 1947. The gulf between academics and curators has not been fully closed but bridges have been built, and communication prospers.

Sincerely yours,

Anthea Jarvis

Fashion Theory, Volume 2, Issue 4, pp.301–314
Reprints available directly from the Publishers.
Photocopying permitted by licence only.
© 1998 Berg. Printed in the United Kingdom.

Cultures, Identities, Histories: Fashioning a Cultural Approach to Dress

Christopher Breward

Christopher Breward is a
lecturer in Design History at the
Royal College of Art, London,
where he teaches on the postgraduate program taught jointly
with the Victoria and Albert
Museum. Author of *The Culture
of Fashion*, he is currently
researching masculinity and
consumption in the nineteenth
century.

The first serious use to which research in historical dress was applied in British academia during the post war period lay in the area of art historical studies. The careful dating of surviving clothing and its representation in paintings was seen as a useful tool in processes of authentication and general connoisseurship. The emphasis on the creation of linear chronologies and stylistic progressions that art historical directions dictated at the time has to some extent influenced the nature of much fashion history writing since. Various approaches have subsequently been adopted following the self-conscious establishment of a school of new art historical thinking in the late 1970s, in which social and political contexts were prioritized over older concerns of authorship and appreciation or connoisseurial value. The arising debates undoubtedly challenged those assumptions that had underpinned the serious study of fashion in the first place. Indeed many of the defining aspects of new art historical approaches, which drew on ideas from Marxism, feminism, psychoanalysis and structuralism or semiotics, encouraged a fresh prominence for debates incorporating problems of social identity, the body, gender and appearance or representation. These are issues that lie at the center of any definition of fashion itself, though it might be argued that their effect has been to nudge concentration away from the artefact towards an emphasis on social meaning (Palmer 1997). Rees and Borzello (1986), in their introductory text on the new art history, use instructive examples of the resulting paradigm shift which had broad implications for the study of fashion history. In their definition of the more cultural scope of new art historical approaches, they state that "when an article analyzes the images of women in paintings rather than the qualities of the brushwork, or when a gallery lecturer ignores the sheen of the Virgin Mary's robe for the Church's use of religious art in the counter-reformation, the new art history is casting its shadow."

However close it came to interrogating the cultural meanings of objects depicted in paintings and other forms of cultural production, the new art history remained largely concerned with issues of represent-ation, the relationship between culture and image. Design history, a relatively young discipline compared to the history of art, has perhaps been able to take on board the complexities of social considerations, economic implications and cultural problems that inform and are informed by objects in a less fixed and self-conscious manner. The relationship between production, consumption and the designed artefact, which has always been central to any definition of the discipline, demands an investigation of cultural context, and is well-suited to the study of historical and contemporary clothing. As design historian Josephine Miller has stated:

> This is a multi-faceted subject and in some ways can be seen to relate to almost every area of design and many aspects of the fine arts. It needs to be placed firmly within a cultural context, against a background of technological and industrial change, literary and aesthetic ideas. In the post-industrial period, the marketing and retail outlets, together with developments in advertising and publishing techniques, have brought a new set of considerations with them. Moreover, the study of dress and its production cannot be separated from women's history (Conway ed. 1987).

Ten years on, the expansion of postcolonial studies and the examination of masculinity and sexuality might broaden her list, but it stands as an indication of the potential held in clothing for a design historical and broadly cultural approach. It is surprising then, that despite its fitness for the field, the study of dress and fashion still remains marginal to wider design historical concerns. This perhaps reflects the discipline's roots in industrial and architectural design practice, with their modernist sympathies. A theoretical and inspirational aid to students of industrial and graphic design, design history as originally taught in art and design colleges tended to prioritize production in the professional "masculine" sphere, re-enforcing notions of a subordinate "feminine" area of interest, into which fashion has generally been relegated. The relatively late establishment of fashion design courses in British art colleges and polytechnics during the 1960s further encouraged a separate provision for contextual and historical studies in clothing and textiles that has probably influenced the semi-detached nature of fashion in the design historical canon ever since.

Related disciplines, including cultural studies and media studies, have arguably taken the politics of identity and appearance—"fashion"—closer to their core, but tend to concentrate on contemporary issues and confine themselves, in tandem with art history, mainly to the study of representation and promotion, using social anthropology and semiotics as tools to define meaning. Significantly, cultural studies finds its history in a literary rather than a visual tradition, and objects of study reflect those roots, existing as texts to be decoded in the present, rather than reflections or remains to be recovered from the past. Whilst much of this work has found its way through to the teaching of fashion students with their more pressing contemporary interests, broader historical issues have remained largely beyond their concern. This brings me to my own limited intervention in the field, a textbook designed to present fashion history in the context of contemporary historiographical debate (Breward 1995). In the face of a potentially confusing and contradictory conflict of interests, I aimed to incorporate elements of art historical, design historical and cultural studies approaches in an attempt to offer a coherent introduction to the history and interpretation of fashionable dress. Used together carefully, these methods promised to provide a fluid framework for the study of fashion in its own right. They could also be set within a wider argument concerning the nature of cultural history generally, which has fostered concepts of diversity rather than prescriptive or narrowly defined readings of historical phenomena. Roger Chartier in his essay that appeared in Lynn Hunt's anthology of new historicist writings (1989) outlines the problems in his discussion of the concepts of "popular" and "high" culture, an area especially pertinent to the history of fashionable clothing and the dynamics of cultural studies:

First and foremost, it no longer seems tenable to try and establish strict correspondences between cultural cleavages and social hierarchies, creating simplistic relationships between particular cultural objects or forms and specific social groups. On the contrary, it is necessary to recognize the fluid circulation and shared practices that cross social boundaries. Second, it does not seem possible to identify the absolute difference and the radical specificity of popular culture on the basis of its own texts, beliefs or codes. The materials that convey the practices and thoughts of ordinary people are always mixed, blending forms and themes, invention and tradition, literate culture and folklore. Finally the macroscopic opposition between "popular" and "high" culture has lost its pertinence. An inventory of the multiple divisions that fragment the social body is preferable to this massive partition.

It is the central contention of much recent work which places clothing in the cultural sphere that clothing has played a defining, but largely uncredited role in the formulation of such differences, microscopic, highly subjective, and deeply personal though their manifestation in dress may be. Fashion therefore requires a method of analysis that takes account of multiple meanings and interpretations. Reductive connections between social influences and fashionable appearance have dogged much fashion history, unaware as it has sometimes seemed to be of the difficulties and complexity of agency. It is here that the new cultural history, in tandem with more recent work in cultural studies, is of use, presenting a more questioning framework which allows for explanations that are multi-layered and open ended. The historians Melling and Barry (1992) have presented a model that acknowledges difference and tensions between new cultural approaches, suggesting a more positive use for the harnessing of divergent directions:

> It would be misleading to present all these changes as moving in harmony and in a single intellectual direction. For example, there is a clear tension between the emphasis laid by some, notably literary critics, on the autonomous power of the text and language, compared to the interest of others in recovering the intentions of historical actors. Put crudely, the former are seeking to deconstruct the identity and rationality of historical actors, while the latter strive to reconstruct them. To some extent we are seeing, within the concept of "culture" as a basis of historical explanation, a revival of the standard sociological debate between "structure" and "action". Should culture be considered as a given system or structure within which past actors are predestined to operate? or does the emphasis on culture place higher priority on human creativity, on self conscious action by the individual or society to change their condition. It would be ironic should this false dichotomy become too well entrenched, since the notion of culture has in many ways been invoked precisely to avoid the need to choose between structure and action, but the danger remains, if concealed by the inherent ambiguity of "culture" as an explanation.

These are useful suggestions for considering the relationship between fashion and culture, though the passage also introduces the deeper problem of pinning down the notion of culture as a neutral descriptive category in the first place. T. S. Eliot (1948) in a famous passage from his "Notes towards the Definition of Culture" could state categorically that "culture . . . includes all the characteristic activities and interests of a people: Derby day, Henley Regatta, Cowes, the Twelfth of August, a cup final, the pin table, the dart board, Wensleydale cheese, boiled cabbage cut into sections, beetroot in vinegar, nineteenth century gothic churches, and the music of Elgar." Ten years later at the birth of cultural studies in Britain as a specific discipline, Raymond Williams (1958) rejected this largely pastoral, romantic and commodified vision to present what he saw as a more inclusive, realist definition of culture that encompassed "steel making, touring in motor cars, mixed farming, the Stock exchange, coal mining and London transport." Forty or fifty years on, both readings of English culture are marked by the effects of nostalgia and the subjective positions of their narrators, but Williams, together with Richard Hoggart (1958), incorporated the idea that culture is a contested and social field in which production and consumption find no easy union and the activities, customs and philosophies of the working class conflict with, or differ from, those of the gentry. Their work established that culture is political as well as aesthetic in its forms and effects.

Between the two positions evolved the formation of a modern school of British cultural studies which aimed to examine precisely the circulation of such constructions and their social power. A purer history of the discipline would trace its roots back to the Frankfurt School and the Institute for Social Research established in Germany in 1923, before moving to the United States, with its largely pessimistic and critical take on the effects of mass culture. There isn't the space here to outline the continuing development of cultural studies as a discrete discipline, and I'm not sure that I could do it the justice it deserves anyway. Graham Turner's recent *Introduction to British Cultural Studies* (1996) provides a more than adequate overview of the historiography and its emergent methods. What I do propose to offer instead is a broad discussion of the key areas in which cultural considerations have made a direct impact on the writing of fashion history over the past decades. These fall largely under the categories of textual analysis (semiotics, film and magazines), the consideration of audience and consumption (ethnography, history and sociology), the role of ideology (hegemony, subcultures and pleasure) and the political question of identities (race, gender, sexuality). These are obviously neither comprehensive nor mutually exclusive divisions, but they do indicate the key ways in which clothing and fashion have finally become a vehicle for debates that now lie at the heart of visual and material culture studies.

Fashion and Signification

The deconstruction of image or product as text lies at the heart of any totalizing definition of a cultural studies methodology. In direct opposition to traditional art and design history and literary criticism methods, cultural studies offers a way of studying objects as systems rather than as the simple product of authorship. Borrowed from European structuralism, most specifically the work of linguist Ferdinand de Saussure (1960), the theory of language "looms as the most essential of cultural studies concepts, either in its own right, or through being appropriated as a model for understanding other cultural systems" (Turner 1996). The structures of language, deployed through speech or text, have been shown to reveal those mechanisms through which individuals make sense of the world: "Culture, as the site where that sense or meaning is generated and experienced, becomes a determining, productive field through which social realities are constructed, experienced and interpreted" (Turner 1996). In the most basic of terms, the science of semiology pioneered by Saussure and later Roland Barthes (1973) offered a more refined mechanism for applying the structural model of language across the wider range of cultural signifying systems, allowing the scholar to examine the social specificity of representations and their meaning across different cultural practices: gesture, literature, drama, conversation, photography, film, television and, of course, dress. Central to this method is the idea of the sign, an anchoring unit of communication within a language system, which might be a word, an image, a sound, an item of clothing, that placed in juxtaposition with other items produces a particular meaning. That meaning is further communicated by the process of signification, the division of the sign into its constituent parts: the signifier (its physical form) and what is signified (the mental concept or associations that arise). Any meaning generated by the sign emerges from the subconscious or automatic relationship of these parts, which is usually arbitrary and culturally relative rather than fixed. It is a meaning that shifts through time and context, so that the ways in which such a shift or relationship might occur are of central importance to cultural studies, because, as Turner (1996) notes "it is through such phenomena that it becomes possible to track cultural change," and also cultural value and cultural associations. Barthes famously attributed the term "myth making" to this production of social knowledge and meaning through the manipulation of the sign, and its cultural and political power is difficult to overestimate.

Fashion historians have of course been utilizing this power for a long time. Everytime the clothing in a portrait is "read" (for its literary associations, the symbolic power of its various textiles and elements of decoration, the value entailed in its material and production that might together offer evidence of status, nationality, age, sexuality or date) representation is being decoded as text, associative meanings combed out and cultural systems established. But the process has rarely been perceived in a self-reflective or critical light. Culture is often taken as an historical given rather than a constructed system in which the portrait or the dress plays its constitutive part. Elizabeth Wilson (1985) must take the credit in her highly influential work on the cultural meaning and history of fashion for questioning and opening up the field. In her aim to ally fashionable dressing with other popular or mass leisure pursuits she has taken the graphic and literary reproduction of dress into a system of mass communication and consumption, hinting at the possibility that more traditional dress history has been toiling unnecessarily in its efforts to use fashion journalism, historical advertising and other popular documentary forms as evidence for actual fashion change or cultural conditions. In her account of the role of clothing in the formation of normative understandings of status and gender, and its capabilities in terms of dissent and deviance from those roles, Wilson has liberated the fashion plate and magazine column from the narrower, linear readings of established dress history:

> Since the late nineteenth century, word and image have increasingly propagated style. Images of desire are constantly in circulation; increasingly it has been the image as well as the artefact that the individual has purchased. Fashion is a magical system, and what we see as we leaf through glossy magazines is "the look". Like advertising, women's magazines have moved from the didactic to the hallucinatory. Originally their purpose was informational, but what we see today in both popular journalism and advertising is the mirage of a way of being, and what we engage in is no longer only the relatively simple process of direct imitation, but the less conscious one of identification.

The conception of fashion as a magical system, which might benefit from textual or linguistic scrutiny, is an area also well tested in the field of film theory and history. The dress historian can draw useful methodological parallels from the way in which authors such as Jane Gaines (1990), Pam Cook (1996) and Christine Gledhill (1987) take examples of cinema and describe the manner in which filmic images interact with women's perceptions of themselves in terms of fashion, sexuality, maternal and marital duty and work. Gaines makes the connections with cultural studies' linguistic and political concerns explicit:

> There is a significant link between the notion of woman displayed by her dress and woman displayed by other representational systems. In addition, one might say that contemporary feminists have understood woman's inscription in the codes of contemporary representation because they themselves know too well what it is to be fitted up for representation. We are trained into clothes,

and early become practised in presentational postures, learning, in the age of mechanical reproduction, to carry the mirror's eye within the mind, as though one might at any moment be photographed. And this is a sense a woman in western culture has learned, not only from feeling the constant surveillance of her public self, but also from studying the publicity images of other women, on screen, certainly, but also in the pages of fashion magazines.

Recent dress history, predicated on a cultural studies understanding of the power of the sign, together with film theory, revels in the ambiguity of fashion and its shifting signifiers, which moves the discipline away from earlier reductive or moralistic approaches. From Thorstein Veblen (1899) through Quentin Bell (1947) to James Laver (1969), historians and commentators from all political persuasions had perhaps taken too many liberties over their ownership of a received understanding of female psychology and supposed predisposition towards luxury, whilst second-wave feminism simply equated fashion with patriarchal oppression. A similarly puritanical strain in early cultural studies echoed a mistrust of fashionable or popular consumption. Such a condemnation of fashion and fashion history implied a dismissal of the women and men who enjoyed its possibilities, and ignored what Gaines has termed "the strength of the allure, the richness of the fantasy, and the quality of the compensation," which their consumption of image and object allowed. Though to follow recent cultural theory on the instability of the sign to its illogical limits presents a particular set of problems that both cultural studies and fashion history have had to address. As Gaines states: "the more extreme contention of post modernist theory—the idea that the image has swallowed reality whole—obliterates the problems endemic to comparisons between images and society. If the image now precedes the real, engulfs it and renders it obsolete as a point of comparison, do we any more need to show how representation is ideological?" (Gaines 1990).

The artificiality of fashion texts and representations would certainly seem open to similar interpretation, so how can they in this sense be tied in to any discussion of inequality, power and manipulation, or the simple actions of consumers themselves? Here the poststructuralist approach of Gaines and others and the broader concerns of cultural studies, with the argument that the image of fashion and femininity is a construction, a textual product of its society, relying only on the reality of the moment, allows for a clearing up of any confusion. The constructed image can be held up for further scrutiny, the construction made clear and the seventeenth-century broadside, the nineteenth-century fashion journal or the twentieth-century film revealed as representational systems. In this way fashion and its associated publicity can be shown to rely on current ideologies, and the "obliterated" problems of image and society reinstated for discussion. The arising affinity between fashion and textual analysis has probably constituted cultural studies' major contribution to the discipline of dress history or, more precisely, dress studies (Craik 1994).

I choose the term "dress studies" over "history" because that contribution has remained largely within the field of twentieth-century and contemporary concerns. The incursion of cultural studies methods into historical discussions of dress has remained more circumspect, and where examples of a convergence between dress, history and the focus of cultural studies on theory and discourse exist, the texts lie on interdisciplinary boundaries, largely on the peripheries of social, literary and art history, and are by authors who often find it necessary to stress their distance both from traditional forms of their own disciplines and from dress historians themselves. The relationship between cultural studies and history has never been a straightforward or easy one, but some of the crossovers have produced interesting studies of historical clothing practices. The source of the disparity between historical and cultural approaches lies in the necessity of the latter to frame itself within a broad theoretical structure. The problem of conceptualizing the social relationships that make up popular cultures defeats contained empirical analyses and therefore led to a split in terms of methodology and theory between structuralists and culturalists at the moment when cultural studies was gaining ground in Britain during the 1960s.

Structuralists viewed culture as their primary object of study, with the forms and structures that produced meaning drawing their attention at the expense of cultural specifics, empirical quantitative evidence and the process of historical change. Culturalists, amongst whom most British social historians of the left placed themselves, resisted this trend as overly deterministic and comprehensive—in a word "ahistorical." For E. P. Thompson (1963) in particular, human agency retained a stronger hold than abstract ideology and the work of British culturalists tended to look inwards to English historical experience rather than outwards to European theory. The two positions rather falsely represent polar opposites for the sake of illustration and more recent work predicated on a broad cultural studies perspective productively knits ideology and experience together through the notion of "discourse." This is a term, owing much to the work of French theorist Michel Foucault (1979), that "refers to socially produced groups of ideas or ways of thinking that can be tracked in individual texts or groups of texts, but that also demand to be located within wider historical and social structures or relations" (Turner 1996). Here the scope for dress history has been wide, as it has for art history and literary criticism, and in my view some of the most exciting examples for a cultural dress history have resulted from this vein. I would offer the work on shopping, department stores and the negotiation of class and gender in the nineteenth century as one manifestation of the approach, incorporating as it does authors as varied as Rosalind Williams (1982), Rachel Bowlby (1985), Valerie Steele (1985), Philippe Perrot (1994), Mica Nava (1996) and Elaine Abelson (1989). It is perhaps significant that only two of these would associate themselves with the discipline of dress history, though all have something to contribute to the development of the discipline.

Pleasure and Politics

Another outcome of the argument between structuralists and culturalists was a repositioning of focus in cultural studies and history that has had further ramifications for the study of fashion. Abstract debates about theory and methodology were superseded in the late 1970s by the opening up of new, previously hidden areas of study and fresh perspectives on old political problems. In social history, those receptive to cultural studies concerns oriented around the formation of the *History Workshop Journal*, which aimed to move discussion away from the academy and into the realm of working people's lives, stressing the importance of feminist and other hidden voices, utilizing the power of oral and non-traditional historical sources that lay outside of the "official record," and claiming that theory might provide answers to social and political problems learnt from the past. In cultural studies, associates of the Birmingham Centre for Contemporary Cultural Studies, founded by Richard Hoggart in 1964, and later directed by Stuart Hall, drew in methods from sociology and anthropology and saw a similar shift in emphasis. Histories of everyday life focused especially on subcultures, examining their construction, their relation to dominant hegemony, and their histories of resistance and incorporation. Much of this work examined the rituals and practices that generated meaning and pleasure within, precisely, that fragment of the cultural field which earlier pioneers from Frankfurt through to Hoggart had dismissed: urban youth subcultures. Dick Hebdige's work on this phenomenon (1979) arguably laid the foundation for several studies of fashion and the young which have fed back in to the dress history mainstream, culminating in both the Streetstyle Exhibition at the V&A (Polhemus 1994 and de la Haye 1996) and the earlier collected essays published under the title *Chic Thrills* (Ash & Wilson 1992).

The whole notion of a "pleasurable" consumption of clothing, which subcultural studies partly raised, is an idea that has now become familiar in fashion histories spanning a broad chronology. But its substance formed the basis of the last political crisis to rock the cultural studies field. The rise of postmodernism, with its questioning of value and authenticity together with the economic effects of Thatcherism and the Lawson boom in the mid 1980s, placed the issue of pleasure and consumption at the center of the cultural studies debate. Summarized by the term "New Times," the discussion was taken up by *Marxism*

Today and signaled, according to Angela McRobbie (1994), "the diversity of social and political upheavals in Britain . . . including the success of Thatcherism, the decline of a traditional working class politics, the emergence of a politics of identity and consumption, and most importantly the challenge these represent to the left." It cannot be easily claimed that fashion history has arisen out of a political consensus in the way that cultural studies obviously has, but nevertheless the implications of the New Times debate have important repercussions for the study of objects which cannot be divorced from questions of status, gender, sexuality and national identity. Though the terms of New Times were complex and inward-looking, the emergence of a new politics of identity and consumption offered genuine opportunities for novel approaches and arguments, represented particularly in works on clothing, fashion, shopping and gender. Recent publications, from Caroline Evans' and Minna Thornton's overview of fashion and femininity in the twentieth century (1989), through to Frank Mort's study of Burton's in the 1950s (1996) or Sean Nixon's examination of menswear and men's magazines in the 1980s (1997), show some residue of the arguments. Any discussion of consumption and its (dis)contents requires precisely the kind of close political analysis that cultural studies methods can provide, and used in conjunction with other, more empirical methodologies its application can often lead to the most provocative and exciting insights.

It is a shame then that the cultural studies slant often seems to raise aggressive or defensive shackles amongst dress historians, as it does amongst historians generally. It is undoubtedly a field riven with disagreements, and coming to a consensus on what the study of culture actually entails is a minefield. In this sense it would be a mistake to isolate cultural studies at all as a desired or necessarily coherent position, more valid than any other. It is an interdisciplinary field where certain concerns and methods have converged. The usefulness of this convergence is that it can enable us to understand cultural phenomena and social relationships that were not accessible through other disciplines, thus enriching our knowledge of an object category (fashion) that has clearly always played a central role in cultural/social processes. It is not a unified field, but one of argument and division as well as convergence, and therein lies its strength and promise. The dress historian Lou Taylor's recent review (1996) of John Harvey's book *Men in Black* (itself a model of interdisciplinary endeavour) offers encouraging signs for the future:

> In Harvey's book we see a very effective shattering of the protective barriers we have erected between academic disciplines. Of course no one person can be "expert" on everything but an open . . . mind . . . set on reading the inner meanings of externals, has demonstrated . . . the great advantages of knocking away the walls of academic protectionism. What is this book? Dress History?

Literary Criticism? Cultural History? Gender Study? Visual Culture? Who cares? Read it.

References

Abelson, Elaine. 1989. *When Ladies Go A Thieving*. Oxford: Oxford University Press.

Ash, Juliet and Elizabeth Wilson. 1992. *Chic Thrills*. London: Pandora.

Barthes, Roland. 1973. *Mythologies*. London: Paladin.

Bell, Quentin. 1947. *On Human Finery*. London: Hogarth.

Bowlby, Rachel. 1985. *Just Looking*. London: Methuen.

Breward, Christopher. 1995. *The Culture of Fashion*. Manchester: Manchester University Press.

Conway, Hazel. 1987. *Design History. A Student's Handbook*. London: Allen & Unwin.

Cook, Pam. 1996. *Fashioning the Nation*. London: BFI.

Craik, Jennifer. 1994. *The Face of Fashion*. London: Routledge.

de la Haye, Amy and Cathie Dingwall. 1996. *Surfers, Soulies, Skinheads and Skaters*. London: Victoria & Albert Museum.

Eliot, Thomas Stearns. 1948. *Notes towards a Definition of Culture*. London: Faber.

Evans, Caroline and Minna Thornton. 1989. *Women and Fashion. A New Look*. London: Quartet.

Foucault, Michel. 1979. *Discipline and Punish: The Birth of the Prison*. Harmondsworth: Peregrine.

Gaines, Jane and Charlotte Herzog (eds.). 1990. *Fabrications: Costume and the Female Body*. London: Routledge.

Gledhill, Christine. 1987. *Home Is Where the Heart Is*. London: BFI.

Harvey, John. 1995. *Men in Black*. London: Reaktion.

Hebdige, Dick. 1979. *Subculture: The Meaning of Style*. London: Methuen.

Hoggart, Richard. 1958. *The Uses of Literacy*. London: Penguin.

Hunt, Lynn (ed.). 1989. *The New Cultural History*. Los Angeles: University of California Press.

Laver, James. 1969. *A Concise History of Costume*. London: Thames and Hudson.

McRobbie, Angela. 1994. *Postmodernism and Popular Culture*. London: Routledge.

Melling, J. and J. Barry. 1992. *Culture in History*. Exeter: Exeter University Press.

Mort, Frank. 1996. *Cultures of Consumption: Masculinities and Social Space*. London: Routledge.

Nava, Mica and Alan O'Shea (eds.). 1996. *Modern Times: Reflections on a Century of English Modernity*. London: Routledge.

Nixon, Sean. 1997. *Hard Looks*. London: UCL Press.

Palmer, Alexandra. 1997. "New Directions: Fashion History Studies and Research." *Fashion Theory*, Vol. 1.3.

Perrot, Philippe. 1994. *Fashioning the Bourgeoisie*. New York: Princeton University Press.

Polhemus, Ted. 1994. *Streetstyle. From Sidewalk to Catwalk*. London: Thames and Hudson.

Rees, A. and F. Borzello. 1986. *The New Art History*. London: Camden Press.

Saussure, Ferdinand de. 1960. *A Course in General Linguistics*. London: Peter Owen.

Steele, Valerie. 1985. *Fashion and Eroticism*. Oxford: Oxford University Press.

Taylor, Lou. 1996. "Men in Black." *Journal of Design History*, Vol. 9.4.

Thompson, E. P. 1963. *The Making of the English Working Class*. London: Penguin.

Turner, Graeme. 1996. *British Cultural Studies*. London: Routledge.

Veblen, Thorstein. 1899. *The Theory of the Leisure Class: An Economic Study in the Evolution of Institutions*. New York: Macmillan.

Williams, Raymond. 1958. *Culture and Society 1780-1950*. London: Penguin.

Williams, Rosalind. 1982. *Dream Worlds: Mass Consumption in Late Nineteenth Century France*. Berkeley: University of California Press.

Wilson, Elizabeth. 1987. *Adorned in Dreams*. London: Virago.

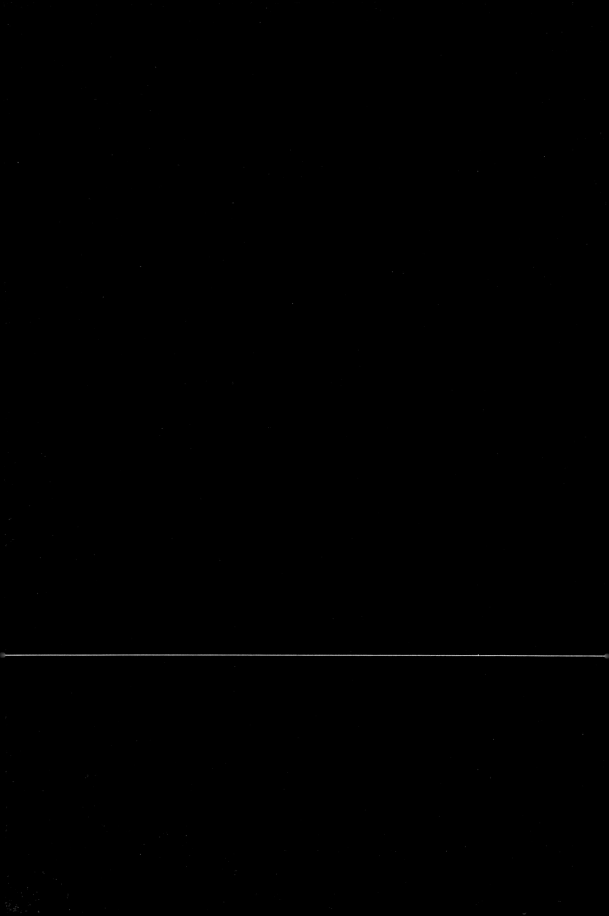

Fashion Theory, Volume 2, Issue 4, pp.315–326
Reprints available directly from the Publishers.
Photocopying permitted by licence only.

Re-Fashioning Art: Some Visual Approaches to the Study of the History of Dress[1]

Aileen Ribeiro

Aileen Ribeiro is Reader in the History of Art at the University of London, and Head of the History of Dress Department at the Courtauld Institute of Art. She is the author of numerous books and articles on the history of dress and has acted as costume consultant to a number of important exhibitions of portraits. She has just finished a book about the representation of dress and appearance in the work of Ingres (to be published by Yale University Press in 1999).

"L'étude de la culture des apparences dans la peinture reste à faire, il y faudrait les competences d'un historien d'art et d'un historien . . ." (Roche 1989: 539).

Over the last decade or so, the study of the culture of clothing in art (the original French title invokes the sense of appearance as well) has been firmly established as one of the essential approaches to dress history; as Roche suggests, such a study requires the skills of both historian *and* art historian.

Most readers will be familiar with the work of James Laver and François Boucher, historians of costume who, in their wide use of different art forms to illustrate their books, established the close links between clothing and its depiction in a range of visual media. It was, however, Stella Mary Newton who pioneered a truly scholarly art historical approach to dress history, through her detailed analysis of clothing in the paintings of the National Gallery. She was the first historian of dress to make the art form (mainly painting) a central point of study, out of which other contexts—social, cultural and political—could develop. Although it is now a truism to state that artists paint the fashions of their own time, and that all their work—even historical, allegorical, religious and mythological scenes—is informed by a knowledge of dress, whether consciously or unconsciously applied, Stella Newton was the first to establish this as fact through a detailed study of the clothing in Renaissance art. The credo which led her, in 1965, to establish the first department at a university for the serious study of the history of dress, is as follows:

> The study of the costume of the past is not a study which can be picked up for the sake of dating a painting, and then dropped. It demands the same detailed research, background knowledge and acute observation combined with imaginative insight, that are essential to the study of art history. It cannot be undertaken without a specialist training, nor can it be successfully carried out except by those who are sensitive to clothes; and it involves the devotion of as many lifetimes as are involved in the study of art history (Newton 1953: 3).

At this point, it is important to stress that the dress historian should *never* look at only one aspect of the subject—whether art object, surviving garments, documentary sources or theory—in isolation; a wide-ranging and comprehensive approach is much more desirable. Individual aspects of the history of dress, *on their own*, have limitations. For example, we can find a great deal of information from documentary material—inventories, invoices, wills, accounts and so on—to help us understand the mechanics of expenditure and consumption, but the terminology of clothing and textile terms is often obscure and confusing, and of limited use to the historian who has no expertise in what the actual garments referred to mean. If we look, to take another example, at literary sources, these give much information as to how people *felt* about their clothes (and those of others), but it is anecdotal and often colored by emotion. When we look at surviving clothing, a knowledge of the fabrics, the cut and construction of costume is clarified; the history of dress in the early periods suffers from the lack of this kind of factual evidence, and is forced to rely on documentary, literary and visual sources. But even when we look at a real garment from the past, we can rarely know how it was worn and with what; internal evidence tells us about textiles and sewing techniques, and sometimes about alterations, but nothing about the person who wore it, and the context(s) in which it was worn.

It is my contention that the visually educated person has a databank of images from all kinds of artistic media to call upon in intellectual life. When, for example, we read a medieval Great Wardrobe account, or a nineteenth-century novel, we conjure up in our imagination, not surviving items of clothing, but images of dress mediated through art.

The history of art and the history of dress have much in common, particularly if by "dress" we mean actual clothing. In both cases the object will be documented (provenance, authenticity, attribution) and analyzed stylistically; its social context will be discussed, its method of production and its reception, and the part it plays in the visual traditions and historical development of the *genus* to which it belongs. In both cases the *study* of the subject—art history, dress history—is as old as civilization itself in the sense that people have always been interested in themselves and the world around them and wished to record their appearance and culture, but the *academic* disciplines of these forms of history are of relatively recent origin.

If we are to consider what has been called the art historical approach to the history of dress, it is first of all necessary to chart some of the main changes in art history itself; what follows is a grossly simplified account in which two major approaches can be identified. The first involves the discussion, as outlined above, of the object; as well as stylistic analysis there is quality assessment or connoisseurship, and typology or classification of shapes/forms within a chronological framework. There is a stress on the work of individual artists and their place in the world, which has been labelled humanistic. Alongside this, early art historians tried to establish a cyclical approach, a notion which implies ascent, apogee and decline; the Renaissance was usually revered as the height of perfection in all the arts. The phrase "Renaissance" man or woman has come to mean someone who excels (or is knowledgeable about) a wide range of arts and literature—fine and applied arts, design, aesthetics, and creative writing; such a person is the antithesis of the expert or specialist. At the same time, however, the Renaissance introduced the notion of hierarchy in the arts, and the division between "high" art and the "applied" arts such as dress. Clearly there are flaws in this concept, in the division between what Plato called the "uselessness" of the represented image, i.e. high art, and the practicality of applied art or craft. Architecture, for example, was regarded as high art, but it was also functional; according to Sir Henry Wotton (1620) it ideally incorporated "commodity" (i.e. practicality) with "firmness and delight." (This is surely an apt description of a well-designed dress or accessory.)

By the middle of the nineteenth century the traditional distinctions between the arts had begun to erode under the influence of such artist–designers as William Morris,[2] and in this century women artists who use fabrics and craftwork to create art which makes aesthetic, social and political connections. Late twentieth-century feminist art historians claim to find the Renaissance classification of art forms demeaning to the status of women in the past, who were largely confined to such traditional applied art forms as needlework, and whose attempts to enter the male world of "high" art were fraught with difficulties. That having been said, there are not many feminist art historians who try to retrieve the lost world of this kind of feminine artistic creativity,[3] nor are there many historians who appreciate the important part played in women's lives by clothing and self-adornment, the most personal and intimate of the applied arts.[4]

The Renaissance emphasis on the idea of genius in the work of the individual artist was modified somewhat in the eighteenth century when the German scholar Winckelmann pioneered the concept of cultural history in which a work of art was related much more to the culture which produced it. It was during this period that antiquarianism flourished, although its origins lay in the Renaissance rediscovery of the past, both history and artefact. Antiquarianism led to systematic classification of objects (the eighteenth century had a passion for the codification of knowledge) and to the creation of museums and specialist collections (including costume).

The second of the two approaches which I referred to earlier arises with our own century, and downplays iconography (the identification of images) in favour of theories and ideologies surrounding the *creation* of the object rather the object itself. As Eric Fernie puts it in his recent work, *Art History and Its Methods: A Critical Anthology*, the "new" art history "shifted the centre of gravity away from objects and towards social context and ...the structure of social power, and from there to politics, feminism, psychoanalysis and theory" (Fernie 1995: 19).[5]

Twentieth century art historians are much more concerned than their predecessors with the arts of their own time, and they often tend to re-create the past in terms of the ideological concerns of the present; this can be liberating or distorting, depending on the writer and on the context. There is less concern with the individual; concepts of abstractionism and expressionism inevitably play down the realistic portrayal of humanity. At the same time psychoanalysis is used to "explain" works of art, and there is more emphasis on demotic art and mass culture. All this has implications for the dress historian. A great deal of recent writing on dress—as the articles in *Fashion Theory* bear witness—involves contemporary fashion and image. In some cases (not all) the authors seem to have little knowledge of, or concern for, the clothing of the past, and consequently no historical context; too many articles, it must be said, are ponderous and often unreadable critiques of the bizarre and the banal, masquerading as research. It is, of course, redressing the balance of much old-fashioned dress history to write about the demotic in clothing, but this should not be at the expense of a knowledge of *haute couture* (the sartorial equivalent of "high" art) and its history; a study of, say, home dress-making is a worthy subject, but it would be much more illuminating if informed by an understanding of the part played by the great designers in establishing contemporary aesthetics and aspirational goals. In the same way the historian of dress should not just concentrate on the nineteenth and twentieth centuries in the belief that the concerns of the last two hundred years are closer to our own, and somehow more "relevant," but should study the subject in the most comprehensive and wide-ranging way, being aware both of the long narrative of clothing, and the many thematic approaches which a detailed knowledge should encourage.

Much of the "new" art history revolves around literary theories which demote the author of a text (or a work of art) and state that each reading (or viewing) is a new and valid re-creation of meaning; there is no longer one true meaning but a series of shifting meanings. So, in terms of art, the focus shifts from the artist/object towards notions of power, gender and so on; using structuralist theory, the art historian examines a work of art via paired and opposing concepts—male/female, light/dark, nude/ clothed, and so on. The artist's own interpretation of his work (in so far as we can ever know it) is only as valid as your "reading" of it, or mine.

Where does this leave the dress historian? Some semiotic theories sit uneasily with visual concepts, and in any case—apropos of the notion of the "authorship" of the text—it is only in the last two hundred or so years that we have any named "authors" or designers of costume. As far as *haute couture* is concerned, the historian of dress will probably always need to assess such productions in the light of individual creation. As for the mass of clothing before the nineteenth century, history is largely silent on the subject of its creation, an extraordinary state of affairs when one considers in particular the sumptuous *ensembles* of the elite as revealed in documentary and visual sources.[6]

With regard to the meanings behind dress, the dress historian, like the art historian, tries to find meanings below the surface content; since the late nineteenth century we have all been aware, as a result of Freud's work, of the hidden complexities behind clothes. In recent years, however, we have run the risk of trying too hard, perhaps, to explain and interpret clothes. It is *because* fashion has for so long been regarded as frivolous that so many writers have rushed to "intellectualize" it in the late twentieth century, with the same fervor that medieval philosophers devoted to wondering how many angels could dance on the head of a pin. In her seminal essay *Against Interpretation* (1964) the American writer and critic Susan Sontag argues that we have been brow-beaten by Marx and Freud, who tell us that events have no meaning without interpretation. She denounces the "itch to interpret," which she defines as "the philistine refusal to leave the work of art alone," arising from fear of real art and "an open aggressiveness" towards it. Her expressed wish is for "a really accurate, sharp, loving description of the appearance of a work of art."[7] The general reader (and many academics also) whose brains have been taxed by over-modish and illiterate writing on art/dress, especially in the field of popular culture, will have some sympathy with Sontag's views, but it must be acknowledged that there *is* no such thing as a "really accurate" and wholly objective experience of *any* work of art. Clearly, in any sophisticated discourse on dress, there is a place for the interpretative element, for clothing is nothing if not about signs and meanings. What we mustn't do is to fasten ourselves to the straitjacket of theory, at the expense of understanding clothing through a complex and overlapping series of assessments and interpretations with the object, what is actually worn, firmly and constantly in mind.

If we take the "text" to be real clothing itself, the notion of re-reading and re-evaluating the object has its limitations, because we cannot gain much perceptual information from the analysis of a single garment. But clothing *en masse*—in the form of an exhibition—is a different matter; a really thought-provoking exhibition is an experience that creates a range of expectations and assumptions, and provokes different forms of appreciation and understanding. To some extent, then, clothing becomes an art form when exhibited *as art*. The contexts in which clothing is exhibited—on a body, on a mannequin, displayed in a case, or suspended from the ceiling like a modern art installation—dictate different reactions and responses. It's important also to note how museum displays are subject to the aesthetics of the time; we put figures into certain poses, and in certain assemblages of costume/accessories to suit *our* notions of the past.

While there is no way we can escape from this, more time and energy seems to be invested in displays of clothing than in exhibition catalogues which can make a major contribution to our understanding of dress. In some cases exhibitions are little more than arrangements of attractive garments (displayed, usually, in a chronological order), with little, if any, critical comment or in-depth contextual discussion of the questions that lie behind and alongside the actual object. After all, art exhibition catalogues consist of a series of essays, even sometimes on clothing, when portraiture is involved.

We need to make a study of artistic sources for dress history central to our subject. The visual arts are the reflection of human history, and carry far more complex intellectual baggage than the actual garments themselves, or the documentary evidence of accounts, invoices and laundry lists. In a work of art, more of the whole picture of clothed humanity is literally revealed; we can see details of the clothes themselves, how they "work" on the body, and what they signify with regard not just to sex, age and class, but to status and cultural aspirations. The art historian Anne Hollander in her classic work *Seeing through Clothes* provides a powerful argument that "in civilized Western life the clothed figure looks more persuasive and comprehensive in art than it does in reality" (Hollander 1978: xi). And again:

"The history of dress or the study of clothes has no real substance other than in *images* of clothes, in which their visual reality truly lives, naturalized, as it were, by the persuasive eye of art" (Hollander 1978: 454).

Such an argument ignores (or at least downplays) the many different and complicated ways in which clothes are indicative of economic pressures, social customs, psychological perceptions, and so on. But it is true to say that the histories of art and of dress are deeply entwined. Both are non-verbal languages and both are social experiences— paintings hang on walls, clothes are displayed on bodies. In our histories, images of humanity are largely clothed images; even with a nude figure there is the implied presence of clothing, and sometimes its ghostly imprint on the body shape.

When, in the Renaissance, there is a revived secular influence on art— an explosion of portraiture and conspicuous consumption of clothing among the elite—we find an impressive involvement by artists not just in the depiction of dress and appearance with a new intensity, but in design itself, of such *objets de luxe* as tapestries, figured silks and jewellery; from the seventeenth century onwards a number of artists began to produce fashion plates, and later on—Monet and Seurat come to mind here—incorporate such images into their work. Over the last hundred or so years there have been particularly close links between art and fashion. Obvious examples that come to mind (and readers will think of many others) include the Spanish painter Mariano Fortuny who settled in Venice at the end of the nineteenth century and turned to the design of unique and beautiful silk garments inspired by the classical and the Renaissance; in this century, there have been well-known collaborative ventures between the designer Paul Poiret and artists (such as Dufy and Matisse) designing fabrics for him, and during the 1930s the imaginative interpretation of Salvador Dali's work into the designs of Schiaparelli.

As with every approach towards a history/histories of dress, some caveats are advisable, for artists are creators as well as recorders of the human appearance; accuracy may be one of *our* concerns but it wasn't always the prime aim of the artist. Over the centuries artists have made a deliberate process of selection in terms of body shape and costume. Stylized figures which are often elongated and distorted can be seen, for example, in a Romanesque manuscript, a sixteenth century Mannerist portrait, an eighteenth century caricature, and so on. Artists will often emphasize certain colors for "artistic" concerns rather than the representation of reality; their palette may at times be limited by what colors were available. They will select certain types of clothing in order to make particular points, such as an emphasis on character traits, or to underline status and accomplishments. In terms of the vocabulary of fashion, they may choose only to paint clothes which are formal or well-established (in society portraiture for example), and we may look in vain for informal costume or new styles of dress and textiles, until they have entered the mainstream. The reverse may be the case in the twentieth century, in that artists will often choose deliberately casual dress or alternative styles of clothing in order to create a more accessible and appealing image.

Artists may also invent costume, and it isn't always easy—especially in periods before clothing survives in meaningful quantities—to distinguish the real from the fanciful. The word "invent" should be used with care, for it is never possible to conjure up a *totally* new style out of the blue and we cannot imagine what we have never seen, nor can the future ever be accurately predicted.[8] Artists' "imagined" garments or draperies are, in fact, usually quite traditional in design, and the characters wearing them reveal the aesthetic of the time by way of gesture and hairstyle, or some small detail like the shape of a sleeve or the placing of a ribbon. We have to be aware, also, of the different types of historical, exotic and allegorical costume which artists use to indicate a world other than their own, such as scenes from mythology or the Bible; such costume can also clothe portraiture in conformity to the cultural climate of certain periods. On the other hand, artists will often make imaginative use

Figure 1
Hugo van der Goes. Seated female saint, 1470s. Courtauld Gallery, London.

This is an example of the artist's use of contemporary costume—the *robe royale*—for a noble or royal saint, who has been tentatively identified as St. Ursula.

of appropriate contemporary costume; we may find, for example, a fifteenth-century Netherlandish painter dressing the noble St. Catherine of Alexandria in court dress, the *robe royale*, or a baroque artist depicting Biblical or mythological characters in contemporary theater costume.

An art historical approach to dress relies on the widest cultural and intellectual background; knowledge of mythology, major religions, great literary works, and a range of artistic production (which may include music, theater, architecture, etc.) outside our own specialist period(s). In a multicultural world, it should encompass non-European art and culture as well.

The painting or other art object is a text to be de-coded; the image becomes a central fact, and no longer just an illustration to a text, but the text itself. We look at a work of art in order to deconstruct the clothing, and then we reconstruct it in the light of our knowledge of *how* clothing works, and its logic in relation to the body, with visual images as the prime source, allied to documentary and literary evidence. Where garments survive, they add valuable information; after all, clothing *as we wear it* cannot be an abstract concept. We cannot just look at clothes as rhetoric and metaphor, but must regard them in an intimate relationship with their wearers. It is through art that we can best perceive the changes in dress and appearance that define fashion; this cannot be evidenced so easily in actual garments unless we are lucky enough to have complete "narratives" of surviving items. Even where these do exist, they present only a fragmented picture, for we cannot be sure exactly how they were worn or in what sequence. For this we have to rely on visual sources, as we do for the whole *ensemble*, as well as for the way accessories were worn, and for gesture and deportment. Again, with regard to documentary material, especially at non-elite level, we only have, so to speak, snapshots of a person's possessions at one point in time, and no sustained evidence of consumption and development over a longer period.

Artists do, in a sense, what the dress historian does; they record, analyze and select or interpret clothing; they provide invaluable testimony to the culture, the manners, the *vision* of the times. *What* they depict and *why* is of crucial importance to anyone seriously interested in the study of dress. The last words on what the ideal historian of dress sees in art will be those of Stella Newton, as sensible and perceptive now as when they were written many years ago:

> Such people do not fall into the error of regarding clothes as painted shapes on canvas; to them, clothes have weight and volume, and mechanisms which allow them to be put on and taken off. The characters of clothes, as they vary from period to period, are revealed in the postures and gestures of the people who wear them. The student of costume, reading gesture as well as dress (in art), imagines himself restricted by the tightness, weighed down

by the heaviness, or released by the amplitude (of the clothes) of the period he is studying, so that in sympathy with the artist who was himself subject to the same conditions, he can see . . . beneath the artist's interpretation of the subject, the fashion of the day (Newton 1953: 25).

Notes

1. This article is a slightly amended version of a keynote lecture given in July 1997 at the "Dress in History" Conference in Manchester.
2. Other examples might include: the artist/designers of the German and Austrian *Sezession* movement at the end of the nineteenth and the beginning of the twentieth century; see also the Omega Workshops founded by Roger Fry in 1913, where members of the Bloomsbury Group of artists designed fabrics, as well as furniture and pottery.
3. An honorable exception is Rozsika Parker's *The Subversive Stitch. Embroidery and the Making of the Feminine*, 1984, London: The Women's Press.
4. Even a very recent work, Amanda Vickery's *The Gentleman's Daughter. Women's Lives in Georgian England*, 1998, New Haven and London: Yale University Press, shows no real understanding *pace* the title, of clothing in women's lives, and avoids any detailed reference to the subject.
5. I am indebted to Eric Fernie's clear and objective discussion in this work of the arguments involved in both traditional and new art history.
6. It is true that there are references in royal and noble accounts in particular to the suppliers of fabrics, and sometimes – though less frequently – to tailors, dress-makers, embroiderers and so on. But there is no sense, as developed from the nineteenth century, of the couturier/couturière who created the complete *ensemble*.
7. Sontag's essay is published in Fernie 1995: 216-222.
8. See Aileen Ribeiro, "Utopian Dress" in *Chic Thrills. A Fashion Reader*, eds. Juliet Ash and Elizabeth Wilson, 1992, London: HarperCollins.

Figure 2
Sir Peter Lely. Portrait of Sir Thomas Thynne, later first Viscount Weymouth, 1670s. Courtauld Gallery, London.

Lely's portrait incorporates the generalized with the particular in terms of the costume. The artist dresses his sitter with studio drapery to indicate the *gravitas* and 'timelessness' of ancient Rome, and underlines his individuality by the use of contemporary details such as the wig, cravat and shirt.

References

Fernie, Eric. 1996. *Art History and Its Methods. A Critical Anthology*. London: Phaidon.

Hollander, Anne. 1978. *Seeing through Clothes*. New York: Viking.

Newton, Stella Mary. 1953. "The Study of Costume as an Aid to the Dating of Italian Renaissance Paintings." *The Bulletin of the Needle and Bobbin Club*, vol. 37: 3–25. New York: The Needle and Bobbin Club.

Roche, Daniel. 1989. *La culture des apparences*. Paris: Fayard.

Fashion Theory, Volume 2, Issue 4, pp.327–336
Reprints available directly from the Publishers.
Photocopying permitted by licence only.
© 1998 Berg. Printed in the United Kingdom.

A Museum of Fashion Is More Than a Clothes-Bag

Valerie Steele

Valerie Steele is Chief Curator
of The Museum at the Fashion
Institute of Technology and
Editor of *Fashion Theory*. She
is also the author of numerous
books and articles.

Because intellectuals live by the word, many scholars tend to ignore the important role that *objects* can play in the creation of knowledge. Even many fashion historians spend little or no time examining actual garments, preferring to rely exclusively on written sources and visual representations. Yet of all the methodologies used to study fashion history, one of the most valuable is the interpretation of objects. Naturally, scholars must also employ standard historical research methods (working in the library), but object-based research provides unique insights into the historic and aesthetic development of fashion. Unfortunately, relatively few historians of dress seem to be aware of the specific methodology devised by Jules Prown, and articulated some years ago in the *Winterthur Portfolio*.

Jules Prown was my professor at Yale University, and I am deeply grateful to him for teaching me how to "read" a dress. In this essay I will attempt to explain his methodology. Prown argues that "style is inescapably culturally expressive" and "the formal data embodied in objects are therefore of value as cultural evidence" (Prown 1980: 197). Or, to put it somewhat differently, "artifacts are primary data for the study of material culture, and, therefore, they can be used actively as evidence rather than passively as illustrations" (Prown 1982: 1).

But how do you go about extracting information about culture from mute clothing? According to Prown, object analysis progresses through three stages, which "must be undertaken in sequence and kept as discrete as possible. The analysis proceeds from *description*, recording the internal evidence of the object itself; to *deduction*, interpreting the interaction between the object and the perceiver; to *speculation*, framing hypotheses and questions which lead out from the object to external evidence for testing and resolution" (Prown 1982: 7).

In his work, Prown cites another model for artifact study proposed by E. McClung Fleming, which I will also briefly describe since it supplements Prown's approach. According to Fleming, "The model utilizes two conceptual tools—a fivefold classification of the basic properties of the artifact" [ie. the history, material, construction, design, and function of the artifact] "and a set of four operations to be performed on these properties." The operations are as follows: 1. Identification (factual description); 2. Evaluation (judgement); 3. Cultural analysis (relationship of the artifact to its culture); and 4. Interpretation (significance) (Fleming 1973: 154).

"Description," Prown insists, "is restricted to what can be observed in the object itself, that is, to internal evidence." It is important to "guard against the intrusion of either subjective assumptions or conclusions drawn from other experiences" (Prown 1982: 7). The first step, therefore, is simply to describe the physical dimensions, material, and fabrication of the object. Tape measures, scales, and magnifying glasses are useful tools. If the object is decorated, describe any overt represent-ations, designs, or motifs. After this, undertake a formal analysis of the object's shape, form, color, and texture. One of the hardest things to judge is how much detail to include in one's description, since a skimpy description provides too little information to work with, but too much detail (such as endless measurements) causes a loss of focus on the object as a whole.

Figure 1
From the Wadsworth Atheneum in Hartford, Connecticut.

Fleming proposes several questions to ask at this stage, above all: What is it? How is it made? Is it genuine, or a fake or forgery?

During Prown's second stage of analysis—deduction—the investigator deliberately injects herself into the picture. Although in most cases it is not possible to try on the clothing in question, you should contemplate what it would be like to wear it. Touch the object, lift it, and otherwise engage in a sensory experience of the object. Next comes intellectual engagement, as you consider what the object does and how it does it. As Prown says, "It is unnecessary to ignore what one knows and feign innocence for the appearance of objectivity, but it is desirable to test one's external knowledge to see if it can be deduced from the object itself and, if it cannot, to set that knowledge aside until the next stage" (Prown 1982: 9). Common assumptions are often wrong, especially in the field of fashion history, where myths can persist unchallenged for years.

In practice, I have found that if students write up the deduction stage, it frequently sounds self-indulgent, as they muse about how they would love (or hate) to wear a particular garment. On the positive side, however, students often become aware during this stage how much of their "knowledge" they must put aside as conjecture or subjective feelings. Ideally, not only do they become aware of their cultural biases, but they can use them to "fuel the creative work that must now take place" in the third and final stage, speculation (Prown 1982: 10).

Although Prown does not explicitly say so, the comparison of objects is also an important part of this methodology. While it is certainly necessary to examine written (and visual) sources, it is also crucial to compare the artifact with others more-or-less like it. Fleming, however, specifies that during the second operation, evaluation, it will be necessary to obtain external information by "comparisons with other objects." Among the questions he raises are the following: Is the artifact typical or unusual? Is it an excellent or a mediocre example of its kind?

When I was a graduate student in Jules Prown's class, I chose to study a woman's dress in the collection of the Wadsworth Atheneum in Hartford, Connecticut. It consisted of a bodice and skirt, both of yellow silk, decorated with dark brown velvet bands and bows. A shirred apron overskirt covered most of the front of the skirt, which was full and back-swept with a train. The velvet bands went vertically up the front of the bodice and down the back, ending in triangular tabs, which were further ornamented with yellow V's and yellow silk tassel fringe. The yellow fringe also decorated the wrists of the sleeves and went along the edge of the overskirt. The velvet bands were echoed by brown diagonals on either side of the underskirt. Three brown velvet bows descended down the front of the overskirt, while a slightly smaller bow decorated the upper center part of the bodice.

Turning from appearance to construction, I noted that the dress was largely machine-stitched, although the decorations were applied by hand. The waistband of the skirt, which measured 23 inches, was held together with heavy hooks and eyes. In my stylistic analysis I observed that substantial quantities of material went into the making of this dress, which was also lined and ornamented, making it rather heavy. The silk was tightly woven, and of a bright "golden yellow" color. The fabric was cut and draped in such a way that the line of the dress was one of exaggerated curves, emphasizing in particular the posterior. The bodice was close-fitting, while the full and voluminous skirt swelled out from a narrow waist, reaching to the floor.

Depending on the questions asked, one chooses various other objects for purposes of comparison. Another student might have analyzed the raw materials and construction techniques used, asking questions about the trade in silk, the chemical analysis of the dye, or the manufacturing costs. Because I was interested in issues of gender and the relationship between clothing and the body, I compared this dress with two other women's dresses from the same period, as well as two corsets, a bustle, and a man's suit, all of which were in the collection of The Costume Institute of the Metropolitan Museum of Art.

The next stage, speculation, involves the framing of questions and hypotheses that then need to be tested against external evidence. In my own work, as I have noted, these questions have tended to focus on gender and sexuality and on the body–clothes unit. Consequently, one of my primary concerns has been cultural attitudes towards the body, and, in particular, the female body. This, in turn, is inextricably connected with cultural perceptions of sexuality and gender. Whatever questions arise must be thought about until it is possible to frame a hypothesis. Since I could hardly help observing that "my" dress would have covered its original wearer from neck to feet, one of my first questions was simply: Why did women's clothes cover their legs? Did they think that the body was sinful? Why did men wear such different clothes? Why was the woman's dress bodice close-fitting and the posterior padded? Was this to emphasize, even caricature, the female silhouette? Obviously, these questions are rather naïve, but they eventually helped me formulate an hypothesis about the sexual significance of high Victorian dress.

In a decade of teaching, I have noticed that this process tends to be difficult for students, who often conclude an essay on the interpretation of objects with a string of unanswered questions. The next step, however, is developing a program of research, thus shifting the inquiry, as Prown says, "from analysis of internal evidence to the search for and investigation of external evidence" (Prown 1982: 10).

Like Prown, Fleming stresses that supplementary information must be obtained from other sources, external to the artifact. However, he describes the process of speculation somewhat differently. Fleming's third operation is called cultural analysis, and it involves the relationship of the artifact to its culture. According to Fleming, "One important form of cultural analysis deals with the functions performed by the artifact in its culture . . . function involves both the concrete and the abstract aspects of the artifact, . . . its various intended uses, and its unintended roles" (Fleming 1973: 156–8). This is also a valid approach, since once one subtracts function, issues of style may come into focus. It is, of course, crucial to be aware that clothing is not simply (or, perhaps, even primarily) "functional," at least not in the concrete sense of the word.

Clothing may, of course, function by telling us something about the wearer.

The issue of clothing messages brings us to another methodology. Whereas with stylistic analysis we are concerned mainly with internal evidence, with semiotics we must go out of the object to understand what each sign means. This is complicated by the fact that a sign stands for something in relationship to somebody, and the meaning of signs changes over time and according to the context and players. The sign (icon) may resemble the object it represents, as an artificial flower sewn on a dress stands for a real flower. The sign (symbol) is assigned an arbitrary meaning. The object that an icon represents may itself be a symbol for something else; a flower, for example, may symbolize spring and, by extension, youth. According to the principles of visual perception, diagonal lines give a greater impression of movement than vertical or horizontal lines. Tassels actually do move. Bows, on the other hand, may be icons for ties or knots, and could, perhaps, symbolize bondage, or, alternatively, presents waiting to be unwrapped. These speculations, unsupported by any external written evidence, helped me at a time when the padding, draping, shirring, and fringe on "my" Victorian dress seemed to give it a disconcerting similarity to a Victorian sofa.

According to Fleming, "Other forms of cultural analysis that may yield significant conceptual generalizations are sampling operations involving a body of related artifacts" (Fleming 1973: 158). In my own work, I have found that simply by *measuring* dozens and dozens of corsets in a variety of collections, I was led to question whether the proverbial 16-inch waist was at all typical of the nineteenth century. This is an example of the importance of artifact study, since the written sources tend to be so polemical. I still recall my outrage when I saw, at an exhibition of Victorian dress, a placard quoting one of the more preposterous letters in the notorious corset controversy in *The English-woman's Domestic Magazine* as though it were a probative and impartial piece of evidence. I wanted to shout at the curator, "Measure the corsets and dresses in this exhibition before you talk to me about 13-inch waists!"

Fleming's fourth operation is interpretation (significance), which he describes as being concerned with "the relations of the artifact to our culture" and, specifically, to "some key aspect of our current value system" (Fleming 1973: 161). This plea for relevance seems, well, relevant to costume exhibitions that have a purely antiquarian focus. I concur even more heartily with his goal of moving "beyond description toward explanation" (Fleming 1973: 158). As another of my professors, Peter Gay, has observed, "the most undramatic work of art presents precisely the same causal puzzles as the eruption of a war, the making of a treaty, or the rise of a class" (Gay 1976: 3).

Back in 1712, my alleged ancestor Sir Richard Steele reported on the idea of a fashion museum. Writing in *The Spectator*, Steele observed that

It was proposed to have a repository builded for fashions . . . filled with shelves, on which boxes are to stand as regularly as books in a library. These are to have folded doors, which being opened you are to behold a baby dressed out in some fashion which has flourished, and standing upon a pedestal, where the time of its reign is marked down. . . . And to the end that these may be preserved with all due care, let there be a keeper appointed, who shall be a gentleman qualified with a competent knowledge of clothes; so that by this means the place will be a comfortable support for some beau who has spent his estate in dressing (*The Spectator*, September 8, 1712).

As the Chief Curator of The Museum of the Fashion Institute of Technology, I am the grateful recipient of just such a position, so I quite agree that fashion museums serve a charitable function. Apart from this, however, the question remains *why* old clothes should be preserved in a museum.

A museum of fashion, like every museum, is a repository for objects from the past. But many people believe that only *some* objects, such as works of art, are worthy of being conserved in a museum. Old clothes would seem too trivial and ephemeral to save. Something of this prejudice is apparent in Steele's facetious comparison of boxes of clothes with books in a library. Books, after all, represent the accumulated wisdom of the ages, while the fashions of the past are often regarded as a monument to the vanity and defective taste of our ancestors. As the fashion journalist Bernadine Morris wrote in *The New York Times*:

A saga of human frailty and vanity was unveiled in the Galleries of the Fashion Institute of Technology when a major exhibition, 'The Undercover Story,' opened yesterday . . . [This exhibition] vividly depicts how far women have gone in the past to distort their bodies willingly in the name of fashion (Morris 1982).

Fashion museums also suffer from a more generalized hostility toward the idea of cultural repositories. Many people are inclined to disparage what they regard as "musty old museums." According to this view, if a museum is not both "fun" and "educational" then it does not deserve support. Articles in the press reveal some doubt whether museum fashion exhibitions fulfill these criteria. On the one hand, museums are accused of over-emphasizing entertainment by putting on popular but mindless fashion shows instead of more socially and artistically significant exhibitions. As a reporter for *The Wall Street Journal* put it:

'Vanity Fair' is a very stylish, very splendid concoction that registers the weight of, say, tulle on the brain. Music floats through the air . . . and the lighting has a theatrical quality. . . . No one

wants to be a . . . spoilsport and take a stern, pedantic approach
to peignoirs and party garb. But couldn't some information be
presented about the various couturiers and their often bizarre
concoctions . . .? (Hoelterhoff 1978).

Yet other observers complain that museum fashion exhibitions are not
fun *enough*, what with darkened galleries and the clothes on static
mannequins rather than living bodies.

The Museum at the Fashion Institute of Technology was formed
initially to provide inspiration and information for fashion designers
and students. Every year, thousands of students and hundreds of
designers and manufacturers utilize the museum's collections, which
consist of approximately 50,000 garments and accessories and about
250,000 textile swatches. These constitute a very important resource
for scholars as well, who, like designers, can benefit from examining
the artifacts that have been so carefully collected and preserved in
museums of fashion. Here I have attempted to present certain models
for analyzing clothing artifacts, thus contributing in a small way to the
justification of the fashion museum.

If fashion is a "living" phenomenon—contemporary, constantly
changing, etc.—then a museum of fashion is *ipso facto* a cemetery for
"dead" clothes. Indeed, many people who are intensely interested in
fashionable clothing (including some fashion designers) are actively
hostile to the very concept of a fashion museum. It is as though they
believe that collecting and exhibiting clothes in a museum effectively
"kills" their spirit. The greater number of fashion designers, however,
are happy to exhibit their clothes in museums, especially if the exhibition
can function as an advertisement for their current styles; which brings
us to another problem.

Fashion has been described as "capitalism's favorite child," and
criticism of fashion exhibitions has correspondingly focused on social
and economic issues. "The Costume Institute has long been a creature
of the fashion and entertainment industries; curatorial policy favors
splendor, exoticism and chic," complained one writer. Even more devast-
ating criticism occurs whenever fashion exhibitions are too closely tied
to the economic interests of particular designers: "Fusing the Yin and
Yang of vanity and cupidity, the Yves Saint Laurent show was the
equivalent of turning gallery space over to General Motors for a display
of Cadillacs" (Storr 1987: 17, 19).

The criticism of particular exhibitions does not, however, mean that
fashion museums as such are doomed to irrelevance or subservience to
commercial interests. The interpretation of objects (also known as
material culture methodology) can provide a powerful tool to address
the problems that frequently beset fashion museum exhibitions—
whether musty antiquarianism or superficial glitz.

References

Fleming, E. McClung. 1973. "Artifact Study: A Proposed Model," *Winterthur Portfolio*, Vol. 9.

Gay, Peter. 1976. *Art and Act: On Causes in History—Manet, Gropius, Mondrian.* New York: Harper and Row.

Hoelterhoff, Manuela. 1978. "Diana Vreeland's Off-the-Rack Favorites," *The Wall Street Journal.* January 13.

Morris, Bernadine. 1982. "Lingerie Exhibition: Vanity's Distortions," *The New York Times*, November 10.

Prown, Jules. 1980. "Style as Evidence," *Winterthur Portfolio*, Vol. 15.

——. 1982. "Mind in Matter: An Introduction to Material Culture Theory and Method" *The Winterthur Portfolio*, Vol. 17.

Storr, Robert. 1987. "Unmaking History at the Costume Institute," *Art in America*, February.

Fashion Theory, Volume 2, Issue 4, pp.337–358
Reprints available directly from the Publishers.
Photocopying permitted by licence only.
© 1998 Berg. Printed in the United Kingdom.

Doing the Laundry? A Reassessment of Object-based Dress History

Lou Taylor

Lou Taylor started her career
as an assistant at the Royal
Scottish Museum, Edinburgh in
1964. She is now Professor of
Dress and Textile History at the
University of Brighton, UK. This
article is drawn from her
forthcoming book for
Manchester University Press,
*Approaches to the Study of
Dress History*.

Introduction

Over the last fifteen years the field of dress history has been subject to
passionate and sometimes acrimonious debate. Within the context of
the history of decorative arts and design, material culture, and museology
and their related cultural theory, the study of dress has undergone the
greatest appropriation and transformation.

The entire world feels it "knows" about the history of clothing. And
indeed why not? The cultural place of dress is so central in any society
that it is of little surprise that art and design historians, literary
historians, economic and social historians, curators, cultural theorists,

private collectors, TV and film directors, fashion designers and tourist organizations have all entered the dress history ring. British television, for example, succumbed to its attractions as early as 1938 when the pioneering BBC television producer, Mary Adams, with the help of England's leading dress historians, James Laver and Dr C. W. Cunnington and the graphic artist Polly Binder, put together the first popular TV series on dress history, *Clothes Line*.[1] In the sixty years that have followed, the subject has become a popular merry-go-round of publications and media events. Amidst all this, it seems an opportune moment now to assess the past, present and future of the work of the object-based dress historian.

Surviving clothing provides researchers and collectors with a powerful tool for historical and contemporary socio-cultural investigation. Yet its use has been bedeviled by a divide of approach that has dogged the study of the history of dress since it emerged over four hundred years ago.[2] It is this divide that forms the focus of this study.

The "Great Divide"

The division, to identify it at its rawest, lies between the object-centered methods of the curator/collector versus "academic" social/economic history and cultural theory approaches as practiced in the university world. The artefact–centered approach, to give just one example, was being mauled only five years ago by Fine and Leopold (1993: 94) as "still . . . in the wholly descriptive 'catalogue' tradition."

Figure 1
Polly Binder, 1939—pages from a private picture diary related to the BBC television series *Clothes Line* of 1938–9; pen and colored inks. Television images of the broadcasting of a back view of a backless 1930s dress caused furious complaints to be sent to the BBC. With thanks to Sally Adams.

This split in approaches has also been mirrored by, and may in part stem from, a related gender divide. Practitioners of the object-based approach were, and still largely are, women, whilst the exact reverse has been the case for the alternative tradition. These problems remained unvoiced in public debate for many years, though they were often discussed privately in both the museum and academic worlds. It is a fact that still today the greater part of those involved in the study of the dress and textile history artefacts are women (and sometimes gay men). There are still only a few full-time dress historians, certainly in Britain. Some are based in the "new" (ex-polytechnic and art-design school) universities, with a very few in the "old" ones. Since we are now having to deal with the hangovers from this divisive history, it is appropriate here to consider how this situation arose.

The History of Dress in Museum Collections

Within European museums, the explanation for the late establishment of "costume" departments dates back to the end of the eighteenth and into the nineteenth centuries, the heyday of the founding of major national museums of art. No major museums collected samples of historical "fashionable" European dress or textiles. The very notion of collecting them seems to have been an anathema to male museum curators, even in museums devoted to "Art and Industry," where logic would expect them to be found.

The prejudice in Britain, and thereafter in the rest of Europe and North America, may well have stemmed from the influences of Sir Henry Cole and William Morris. Cole, who was both the instigator of the 1851 Great Exhibition and, a year later, the founding Director of the Museum of Manufactures in Marlborough House, London (ultimately to become the Victoria and Albert Museum), did show an interest in the design of dress fabrics. Editorial within his own *Journal of Design and Manufacture* regularly commented on fashion fabrics but rarely on dress. This could have been due to the fact that women's fashions were not yet being "manufactured" at a ready-to-wear level; but for whatever reason, this absence was carried over into the collecting policy of the new museum.

William Morris (1986: 234–5) also had a strong involvement with the textile collecting policy of the museum. We know from *News From Nowhere* that he considered women wearing the bustled styles of the 1870s and 1980s to look unnatural, "bundled up with millinery . . . upholstered like armchairs." He recommended a style "somewhat between the ancient classical costume and the simpler forms of the fourteenth-century garments." It seems highly unlikely therefore that he would champion the museum as a repository for Paris-inspired fashionable dress.

Thus a hostile attitude to the collection of seasonally-styled European fashion for women became enshrined within the museum's collecting policy from the very start. A few clothing items did creep in—a Paraguayan shirt in 1854,[3] and items of sixteenth-, seventeenth- and eighteenth-century dress that were collected from the late 1860s onwards. The 1875 catalogue of the museum's Industrial Art collections had no section on costume. Gloves, coifs, purses and a few complete garments were accepted because of their weave, print and embroidery techniques rather than for any interest in cut or seasonal styling.

Figure 3
Case of eighteenth-century dress, from the Talbot Hughes collection, given to the museum in 1913, and on display in the Victoria and Albert Museum; from Harrods Ltd. (no date), *Old English Costumes selected from the collection formed by Mr Talbot Hughes, a sequence of fashions through the 18th and 19th centuries, presented to the Victoria and Albert Museum, South Kensington,* with thanks to Guy Fullerton.

However, by 1914, as illustrations to the museum's catalogue of their Talbot Hughes donation shows, eighteenth-century clothing was finally displayed in a remote upper corridor of the museum. Charles Gibbs-Smith (1976) confirmed that this negative policy continued into the 1930s. "Museum officials . . . regarded some artistic and allied subjects with a certain suspicion, especially the study of historic costume, which most of the staff thought of only as a sort of rather unholy byproduct of the textile industry." This latter term gives the key to this continuing scorn. In the eyes of male museum staff, fashionable dress still only evoked notions of vulgar commerciality and valueless, ephemeral, feminine style.

Figure 4
Illustration from *Old English Costumes selected from the collection formed by Mr Talbot Hughes, a sequence of fashions through the 18th and 19th centuries, presented to the Victoria and Albert Museum, South Kensington:* blue silk coat of about 1780.

ST. MARGARET'S CHURCH, BRIGHTON,
WHICH IS GOING TO BE TURNED INTO
A MUSEUM OF COSTUME
See letter: Church into Museum

Figure 5
St Margaret's Church, Brighton
in 1958, one of the homes
planned for Doris Langley
Moore's costume collection.
Courtesy of *Country Life*.

It was not until the 1950s that attitudes began to change on both sides of the Atlantic, and only then because professional women curators began to be appointed. Pioneering work was undertaken in England by Madelaine Blumstein/Ginsburg and Natalie Rothstein at the Victoria and Albert Museum, Anne Buck at the Gallery of English Costume at Platt Hall, Manchester and Doris Langley-Moore. Natalie Rothstein believes that in Britain the employment of professional women dress/textiles curators came about simply because of the passing of an equal opportunities act within the British Civil Service in the mid-1950s.[4]

However, even once in post Madelaine Ginsburg (1962: 17) wrote bitterly in her own gallery notes for the newly rearranged Costume Court in 1962 that "unfortunately the fashion story reflecting the present age of the atom bomb, the affluent society, synthetic fabrics and mass production, is not represented in the museum's collection." Roy Strong, once appointed museum director, made a profound commitment to raising the hierarchical status of the dress collection within the museum. Amy de la Haye believes that it was the 1971 exhibition, *Fashion, an Anthology by Cecil Beaton*, held during his regime, that "really put fashion on the map at the V. and A."[5] Beaton collected over 500 examples of twentieth-century couture garments and accessories for this show.

Figure 6
Press cutting from local Brighton newspaper in 1958, discussing the row over the development of Doris Langley-Moore's Museum of Costume in the town.

Museum of Costume Idea Waste of Money

————◆————

TORY COUNCILLOR PREFERS FLATS

BRIGHTON is throwing money away to bring the Museum of Costume to the town, a Tory councillor, Mr John Ireland, declared at a public meeting on Thursday night.

Referring to the Old St. Margaret's Church in St. Margaret's-place, which, it is intended, will house the Museum, Councillor Ireland commented: "I'm not in favour of spending £20,000 to put the building in proper condition.

"Some people regard it as a fine piece of Regency Architecture. That may well be. But it has served its purpose. I think it should be demolished and the site used for a block of flats. I'm quite sure the Council are wasting public money by deciding to convert it into a museum."

Councillor W. Clout (Conserva-

It took Doris Langley-Moore fifteen years of desperate struggle to establish a home-base for her magnificent costume collection. In the mid-1950s the town of Brighton, on the south coast, made her a series of promises over the use of a pretty Regency church for her museum, but chose finally to erect a luxury block of private flats on the site instead. Her collection was saved by the offer of the Assembly Rooms at Bath, when refurbishment of wartime bomb damage was finally completed. *The Museum of Costume* finally opened in 1963.

The struggle to found the costume museum of the city of Paris dates right back to 1906, when the Société de l'Histoire du Costume was established (*Bulletin de La Société de l' Histoire du Costume*, 1907.) Efforts ebbed and flowed until finally in 1977, after a lifetime of disappointments, Madeleine Delpierre finally achieved the conversion of the Duchesse de Galliera's neo-Renaissance mansion, the Palais Galliera, into a custom-built dress museum, now the *Musée de la Mode et du Costume de la Ville de Paris*. Yvonne Deslandres also struggled for over thirty years to find a base for François Boucher's Union Français des Arts du Costume collection, founded in 1948. It was not until 1997 that this found a final haven as the *Musée de la Mode et du Textile* in the Palais du Louvre, Rue de Rivoli.

In New York from the late 1920s, four women, Irene Lewisjohn and her sister, Alice, with the help of Aline Bernstein and Polaire Weissman, put together a collection of ten thousand items of dress. After much campaigning this was finally added to the Metropolitan Museum collection in 1944, forming the base of the Costume Institute (Druesdow 1987). It was Stella Blum who propelled this collection into the international arena through her period of strong and innovative curatorship.

Figure 7
Bomb damage to Assembly Rooms, Bath, 1942, later the home of the Gallery of Costume; courtesy of the Museum of Costume, Bath.

Figure 8
Early catalogues from the
Gallery of English Costume,
Platt Hall, Manchester, 1950s
and the Union Française des
Arts du Costume, Paris,
1968–70.

Ethnographical dress collections

The history of the collection of ethnographical dress is a quite different
story. Collected from the seventeenth and eighteenth century onwards
as representative of the cultural artefacts of the Noble Savage and the
exotic "Other," examples date back to the earliest days of the Cabinets
of Curiosity. Collectors included Christoph Weickmann (1617–81) a
sophisticated patrician/merchant from Ulm in Germany, a tulip cultivator
and a telescope designer. He had built up his fortune with professional
trading contacts into Africa. His personal collection, begun in 1653 or
1654, covered the usual Cabinet of Curiosity interests in stuffed animals,
fossils, and bizarre and exotic artefacts. What is not usual is that he
published his own catalogue, *Exoticophylacium*, in 1659 and that both
it and some items from his collection have survived.

Dr. Michael Roth (1991 and personal communication, 6 September
1995) of the *Ulmer Museum* has been gathering information on the
history of this *Kunst-und-Wunderkammer* (wonder room of art), noting
the survival of two examples of men's cotton robes from West Africa,
both indigo-dyed. They are now identified as coming from Allada in
the Republic of Benin. These two mid-seventeenth-century African robes
may be among the oldest examples of "collected" museum garments.

Thus, unlike the study of fashionable Western European dress, the
collection of clothing artefacts was included in rather than excluded from
the field of ethnography from its very beginnings. Nonetheless, from

the 1970s many specialists, especially women, were voicing the view that analysis of cloth and clothing had been marginalized within the field of ethnography. Ronald Schwarz (1979: 28) in an entertaining but angry article, "Uncovering the Secret Vice: Towards an Anthropology of Clothing and Adornment," declared that "clothing is a subject about which anthropologists should have much to say yet remain mysteriously silent." Schwarz (1979: 41–2) directly raised the issue of the perceived male anthropologists' bias against the study of dress. He quoted Tom Wolfe: "Amongst the Big Men, clothing is a taboo subject. They don't want it known they even care about it . . . Sex, well all right, talk your head off. But this, these men's clothes."

Annette Weiner and Jane Schneider (1989: 25) raised the same problem ten years later in their introduction to *Cloth and the Human Experience*. Recognizing that cloth produced by women makes a centrally significant contribution to ritual and social life in so many cultures, they ask why ethnographers (by implication here meaning male ethnographers) "often overlook this possibility, whether from a disinterest in women's activities, or in fibers and fabrics (as distinct from food) or both." They believe that this failure has led to the use of "simplistic and inadequate" analytical ethnographical categories. This in turn has mistakenly pushed women and their cloth and clothing manufacture into a "domestic" social corner. This gendered debate still continues.

The "Great Divide": The Object Versus Academia

That there was a profound academic prejudice against the field of dress history was a view already voiced in the early nineteenth century. In 1815 Dr. Samuel Rush Meyrick and Charles Hamilton-Smith wrote that costume history was burdened with "the intemperate and hasty charge of carrying with it the inferiority of not being worthy of consideration of a man of letters." Some working in the subject today still hold to this view.

Since the inter-war period, university departments of economic and social history who based their textile history research methodologies on firmly established economic and social history approaches excluded examination of the actuality of the fabrics they were assessing. Thus very little object-based research was undertaken. When it was, it failed almost totally to address the significance of issues of fashion, style and seasonal change.

The Economic and Social History Approach

One well-known and typical example of the economic history approach to textiles will serve here to encapsulate this whole debate, William

Reddy's rigorous 1984 study *The Rise of Market Culture—The Textile Trade and French Society, 1750–1900*. He discusses the significant role played by textile production within the major industrial transformation processes of the period. He discusses the realization amongst calico manufacturers that "slight decreases in price brought large increases in consumption," which in turn led producers in the direction of new consumers and new profits. This process included "supplying peasants and artisans with bright, pretty, abundant cloth whose price moved steadily downward" (Reddy 1984: 88 and 91). There are no illustrations of cloth and there is no object-centered debate to show how these "downward" price differences might have been achieved with simpler, less seasonally dictated designs. Thus evidence that an object-based textile historian would consider vital to this debate is missing completely.

In this Reddy is no worse than other historians. Until about ten years ago the specific artefact history of Western European feminine fashions and fashion fabrics was largely deemed to be unworthy of the attention of "big" historians. In the field of economic textile history these were invariably male. To give another example, in *Textile and Economic History* (Harte and Ponting 1973) out of its fifteen chapters only two were written by women. One was Joan Thirsk, Reader in Economic History and Fellow of St Hilda's College, Oxford. Her 1973 article dealt with the economic impact of style on the knitted stocking industry. Interestingly, in it she attacked her male colleagues for according fashion such "a lowly place" in academic research (Thirsk 1973: 50).

From the mid-1970s Negley Harte, an economic historian from University College London, mounted a concerted campaign to develop the specific study of dress and its related textile history within his own academic field. In 1976 he wrote: "Given the nature of the climate [in Europe], the demand for clothing has taken second place only to the demand for food as a fundamental factor in the economy of the continent for many centuries ... The production, the distribution and the consumption of textiles cannot therefore be ignored by any serious economic and social historian of Europe" (Harte 1976: 198). In 1991 he repeated that "economic historians ... have shied away from attempting to address their statistical questions to clothes themselves" (Harte 1991: 277).

Object-based Research

Object-based research focuses necessarily and unapologetically on examination of the details of clothing and fabric. This process depends upon a series of patiently acquired, specialized skills. From identification to conservation, from display to interpretation, these are skills that have been underrated by many economic, social and cultural historians. Curators and conservators become expert at professional specialist care over cleaning, repairing, washing, pressing, storing and displaying clothing. These are all skills that society at large still considers very feminine domestic occupations—almost, one might say, like doing the laundry. Yet identification and dating is only possible through precise knowledge of intricacies of cut, trimmings, making-up and fabrics used in clothing of every period and by every class and culture.

Excluded from the higher ranks of the museum and university worlds because of these negative perceptions of their field, object-based specialists, mostly women, have had to endure both a lowly status and a lack of proper respect for their profession. Anne Buck, Keeper of the Gallery of English Costume at Platt Hall, Manchester from 1947 to 1972, has devoted her entire professional life to raising the status of dress curatorship and research. She has always drawn object-based research into its wider social context, and has done so with exemplary skill but it was a struggle (Hart 1980 and Buck 1991, 1996). She noted in 1958 (Buck 1958: 3) that "costume takes a very minor place amongst the arts, and in museums of the applied arts examples appear as illustrations of the arts of weaving, embroidery or lace making."

The main criticism levelled at object-based dress historians has centered on their "descriptive" concentration on the minutiae of clothing. Fine and Leopold in 1993 dismissed a series of dress studies by "the Cunningtons, De Marly, Ewing, Kidwell, Ribeiro, Taylor, Tozer and Levitt" as being "in the wholly descriptive 'catalogue' tradition of costume history, which typically charts in minute detail over the course of several centuries the addition or deletion of every flounce, pleat button or bow, worn by every class on every occasion." In their own discussion of the importance of clothing in the context of consumption, they acknowledge dress as an increasingly powerful economic and social force in the First World over the last one hundred years. They also stress that approaches to consumption should be "based on the recognition of distinct systems of provision across commodities." They explain the need for "discussion of the private versus social (or individual versus collective) nature of consumption," which has to be "sensitive to differences in the way objects are produced, distributed, consumed and interpreted as discussion that sets supply against demand" (Fine and Leopold 1993: 94, 299–304).

No dress historian would disagree with any of this but would add that without precise analysis of "every flounce," where would the historian find the information that would enable recognition of these "distinct systems of provisions"? How are coded cultural readings of "the private versus social" nature of consumption to be made except through meticulous study of these details?

Approaches such as those taken by Reddy, Fine and Leopold confirmed a strong feeling within the international community of dress historians that their methodological approaches had not been accepted in "academic" circles.

The Debate Starts

The "great divide" between object-based and "academic" approaches became public in Britain in a debate triggered by Negley Harte in his role as Chairman of the Pasold Research Fund through the 1980s and 1990s. He stated in 1977 that, as a field of study, the history of dress was

> backward . . . the history of costume as conventionally perceived is wanting in at least two important respects. . . . Firstly clothing is generally quite inadequately related to wide matters of concern to the historian of social change and movements in the standard of living for example or to price levels, patterns of expenditure and consumption. Secondly, and more particularly, dress is studied almost entirely separately from textiles, from the textile trades and from the changing technology of textile production. Until such dimensions have been added costume history is in danger of aspiring no higher than to antiquarian status (Harte 1977: 183).

In 1991 he renewed his attack, describing the typical work of historians of dress as merely "a lucky dip" of "artistic, psychological or sociological concerns" with the subject (Harte 1991: 277).

The problem was also recognized from the curatorial side. In 1984 Jane Tozer, a curator at Platt Hall, Manchester, made a tough address to the 1984 Costume Society Symposium. Appealing for broader approaches, she declared "we should seek to relate dress to its historical, artistic, social and economic context . . . It is unfortunate if these disciplines seem at times to be opposing camps. The standard texts of the future will come from a synthesis of these views" (Tozer 1986: 16).

The two divided approaches to dress and textile history are very evident in the professional British journals, *Costume*, from 1967 and *Textile History*, founded in 1968. The object-centered journal, *Costume*, edited by Ann Saunders, has always aimed to appeal to both the expert and the enthusiast, all mostly women. In 1976 there were 20 women to 5 men on the committee, with 6 articles by women and 3 by men in the journal. Close examination of many *Costume* articles shows that this journal does indeed deal with "flounce and frill," but that it has also dealt with the full social range of consumers, from the aprons of Cullercoats fisherwomen through to the garments of Royalty (see for example Hamer 1984 and Wardle 1997). Close reading of *Costume* makes it clear that this journal has always considered clothing to lie within the embrace of social history, though it does not as a policy provide space for in-depth social history research *per se*. As early as 1973 costume curator Avril Lansdell outlined the social history-related costume collecting policy of Weybridge Museum in Surrey, explaining that clothes "play their part in the unfolding of the local story, adding a new dimension to historic research" (Lansdell 1973: 3). *Costume* only occasionally includes articles on ethnographical dress, and rarely deals with theories dealing with the cultural significances of clothing. The inclusion in the 1997 edition of the text of a lecture on "Street Style" given by Caroline Evans (Evans 1997: 105–10) of Central Saint Martins College of Art and Design, London is an encouragingly progressive move for this journal.

Support for *Textile History* has stemmed from university economic and social history departments. Over the first twenty years of its existence the journal's fourteen-strong editorial team and contributors were mostly male. This is not surprising, given the gender imbalance of staff teaching economic history in British universities. In 1985–95 Negley Harte organized an international series of multi-disciplinary conferences whose findings were published in the journal. In a barrier-breaking move in the early 1980s, Dr. Aileen Ribeiro, Director of the Courtauld Institute's MA course in Dress History, was invited to be a Governor of the Pasold Research Fund, which supports this journal. Looking back over its twenty-six years of publication, it is clear that the aims and activities of *Textile History* have now shifted a long way from their 1968 Eurocentric, male, economic history base.

This change in attitude, happily reflected in a whole range of new research published over the last ten years, is thus centered on the use of multi-disciplinary approaches. This has also been promoted in the USA by Nancy Rexford, for one, in her 1988 article "Studying Garments for Their Own Sake: Mapping the World of Costume Scholarship."

Positive Developments in the International Museum World from the 1980s

Innovative use of such methodologies within the interpretation of fashionable dress has become evident in museum displays and publications in Europe and in North America over the last ten years. In the USA Elizabeth Anne Coleman's *The Opulent Era* of 1989 laid down a benchmark followed later by others. She exposed the essential relationship between garment, manufacture and consumption in the world of couture clothing produced by the Paris salons of Worth, Doucet and Pingat. Another challenging example was set by the City of Paris's *Musée de la Mode,* Palais Galliera. In 1990, for example, the exhibition, *Femmes: Fin de Siècle, 1885–1895* included the expected examples of elegant Paris couture clothing, but added to these garments from the great Paris department stores (also astonishingly smart) together with an explanation of retailing processes. Further, sportswear, mourning dress and even the Paris styles worn at the Meiji court in Japan were also included. The influence of Japan on Western fashion and textiles was the focus of the spectacular, carefully documented 1996 exhibition,

Japonisme et Mode, drawn from the collections of the Costume Institute at Kyoto. Another first was Valerie Guillaume's 1993 exhibition at Palais Galliera on the work of the couturier Jacques Fath. This was the first to tackle openly and factually the reality of the continuation of the Paris couture trade under Nazi Occupation. She showed not only the clothing made during those nightmare years, but also who wore them and where.

In 1993 in London, the Victoria and Albert Museum's collecting policy was widened radically when the decision was made to hold the controversial *Street Style* exhibition. Curated by Amy de la Haye, this opened in 1994, showing hundreds of outfits representing post-war British and American young, radical, sub/counter-cultural clothing. This show undoubtedly catapulted this national institution into widening its definition of collectable artefacts and into addressing the realities of late-twentieth-century British design processes.

Despite such developments, however, Naomi Tarrant, Assistant Keeper of Dress at the Royal Museum of Scotland in Edinburgh, for one, still believed in 1994 that even "in museums, costume is at present being marginalized" (Tarrant 1994: 12).

Positive Developments in the Academic World since the Mid-1980s

In the academic world of economic and social history, a wave of fresh new multi-disciplinary research on clothing has also been undertaken by both male and female academics over the last ten years. In the introduction to their boundary-crushing 1993 study *Consumption and the World of Goods* (Brewer and Porter 1993.1) John Brewer, a historian from UCLA and Roy Porter, from the Wellcome Institute for the History of Medicine in London, avowed their interests in consumption and artefacts. They declared that it was "high time for 'big history' to address one of the special features of modern Western societies . . . the capacity to create and sustain a consumer economy, and the consumers to go with it."

It is out of this recognition of the essential worth of consumption studies and analysis of the actuality of specific "goods" that a new generation of dress (and its related textile history) research is emerging. Much of this is centered on early periods, such as Margaret Spufford's 1984 *The Great Re-clothing of Rural England* and Beverly Lemire's *Fashion's Favorite: The Cotton Trade and the Consumer in Britain, 1660–1800* of 1991 and *Dress, Culture and Commerce, the English Clothing Trade before the Factory, 1660–1800* of 1997. Lemire, Professor of History at the University of New Brunswick, Canada, applies contemporary material cultural approaches using local and national archives, press reports, tailors' order books, advertisements and so on.

A seminal example of this methodology is to be found in Amanda Vickery's 1993 *Women and the World of Goods: A Lancashire Consumer and Her Possessions, 1751–81*. By researching in Lancashire archives, Vickery has destroyed for ever many "given" assumptions held in the past by some historians (mostly male) that women's role as consumers of ephemeral fashion was of little economic or social significance. Vickery researched the life and possessions of Mrs. Elizabeth Shackleton, who lived within lesser gentry circles in Lancashire. Vickery significantly concludes that her own "reassessment of consumption paves the way for the historical reclamation of the female consumer" and that this "challenges a long-held disdain for the study of 'fashion' and opens the door on one of women's most important historical roles, as managers or participants in household consumption strategies," emphasizing the personal rather than the institutional (Vickery 1993: 278).

Anne Smart Martin (1993: 141–57) affirmed that "material objects matter because they are complex, symbolic bundles of social, cultural and individual meanings fused onto something we can touch, see and own." If ever there was an answer to Fine and Leopold's condemnation of artefact research, it lies here in Smart Martin's words. Pierre Bourdieu too (1989: 231) acknowledges the importance of things, explaining that "cultural objects, with their subtle hierarchy, are predisposed to mark the stages and degrees of the initiatory progress which defines the enterprise of culture."

These new approaches, boosted by the work of Daniel Miller (1987 and 1995a, b), Grant McCracken (1988), Igor Kopytoff (1986) and others, have become a positive and guiding force within the revitalization of dress history. Porter, Brewer, Breen, Styles, Vickery and Lemire have all still to take the final step of assessing details of surviving artefacts in their research. Nonetheless, it is clear that high levels of multi-disciplinary good practice, which use object–based research as a base point, are now emerging from both sides of the great divide and at an international level.

Recent Examples of Good Practice Using Multi-disciplinary Approaches

New generations of women ethnographers, such as Justine Cordwell (Cordwell and Schwartz 1979), Annette Weiner and Jane Schneider (1989), Ruth Barnes (Eicher and Barnes 1993) and Joanne Eicher (Eicher and Barnes 1993 and Eicher 1995) have also made fresh and important contributions to their field by placing analysis of cloth and clothing fully into its related cultural and historical settings. It is clear that historians dealing with "fashionable" dress can learn a great deal from these ethnographical approaches.

The work of the French ethnographer, Beatrix Le Wita (1994), a member of the *Centre d'Ethnologie Française*, provides one excellent example. This 1994 research caused a public *frissonne* in the French media because Le Wita's ethnographical focus was the young, wealthy bourgeoisie living today in the western suburbs of Paris rather than a tribal group in Africa or South America. Significantly, she introduces her research methods by emphasizing how important it is, to use Balzac's words, "to pay attention to the 'little details.'"[6]

Le Wita notes that "the history of costume reveals how the bourgeoisie has repeatedly replaced the aristocracy's ostentatious distinguishing marks with marks that are more restrained, more discreet, though no less formidable in terms of symbolic effectiveness." Focusing on young married women, she concluded that they used "almost imperceptible make-up [which] reinforces the general impression of moderation or neutrality [conveyed] by these young women." Even their bourgeois jeans were neutral in style, "neither too tight, nor too baggy, nor too long, nor too short." Le Wita concluded that clothing plays a vital role, whereby "the whole persona of the bourgeois, from appearance to voice modulations, is thus imbued with the values and cultural schemata of the group."

Interestingly, it is at this point that Le Wita's ethnographical approaches and the material culture methods of Daniel Miller overlap. Miller (1995: 143 and 157) also stresses that research needs to take careful cognizance of artefacts. "Within the study of increasing commodification," he writes, "perhaps the most interesting literature has examined how key items in modern consumption are used to objectify, and thereby under-stand, the nature of modernity as a social experience."

The American social historian Barbara Schreier (1994: X1, 2, 5) offered an excellent example of multi-disciplinary practice through her meticulously researched use of clothing artefacts in the 1994 exhibition *Becoming American Women: Clothing and the Jewish Immigrant Experience, 1880–1920*. The exhibition and accompanying catalogue included assessment of peasant clothing bought over from Russia, an early twentieth-century Orthodox *sheitel* wig and examples of the Americanized fashions favored by younger Jewish women in the 1900–1915 period. These objects were each placed within their precise individual biographical settings with the help of a full range of photographs, period and oral history comments, and surviving related ephemera.

Schreier's aim was to demonstrate how these artefacts explain "explicitly the experience of Eastern European Jewish women" and how they epitomize "the corrosive character of immigration and duality of identity that corrosion can create in the those who suffer it." The whole concept of the exhibition and its accompanying book is based on a sharp appreciation of "the importance of dress as a sign of cultural mingling," secondly, its role as "a force for the sustaining of cultural values," and thirdly as "an identifiable symbol of a changing consciousness."

In 1990 Natalie Rothstein, Keeper of the Department of Dress and Textiles at the Victoria and Albert Museum, also produced a methodologically significant artefact-based book and exhibition. These assessed the museum's collection of eighteenth-century French and English silk brocades in the context of the trade organization of weavers, designers, and merchants, the actuality of consumption and even issues of national identity in silk design. Artefacts on display included the silks, account books, and samples and wonderful portraits of male and female consumers from both sides of the Atlantic wearing Spitalfields silks that exactly matched the garments on show. Rothstein included a sensitive and astute analysis of the Englishness of Spitalfields silk design at one moment of high achievement, the 1735–45 period. This account remains unequalled, because it was based on a lifetime of research into the design details of these specific silks.

Research by Alexandra Palmer (1994 and 1997), now Curator of Dress and Textiles at the Royal Ontario Museum, Toronto (already acknowledged in volume 1/3 of this journal), successfully applied material cultural methodologies to the style, manufacture, retailing and consumption of couture clothes worn in Toronto in the 1945–63 period. Palmer explodes a series of "taken as read" assumptions that will please Amanda Vickery. Palmer proves conclusively that most British Canadian couture consumers in the 1950s did not see their expensive dresses as passing luxuries but as long-term investments, that their Parisian garments were sometimes moderated to suit their Canadian tastes and that they purchased couture, above all, as a peer-group "social uniform" and as a cultural requirement.

Margaret Maynard, from the Department of Art History at the University of Queensland, in her 1994 study *Dress as Cultural Practice in Colonial Australia*, also used clothing analysis to debate the issue of national identity. After discussing men's dress from the bush and the goldfields and its associated mythologies, Maynard concluded that "the concept of an Australian national type, a rugged male wearing bush hat, moleskins, shirt and boots, was a construct of the 1840s and 1850s and given additional romantic gloss by the popular and high art imagery of the 1880s and 1890s." She adds, interestingly, that "as Australia moves towards republicanism . . . Australians of the 1990s seem more anxious than ever to turn to the perceived values of the bush as a source of comfort and reassurance" (Maynard 1994: 179 and 181).

Caroline Evans and Minna Thornton (1989), Jennifer Craik (1994), Christopher Breward (1995) and Frank Mort, to give a few examples, have all recently also produced invaluable contributions to the analysis of contemporary clothing. The 1990s has thus witnessed radical and innovative developments within the field of dress history—reflected also in the pages of this journal.

Conclusion

To conclude with the words of a literary historian, John Harvey (1995: 17), this fusion of multi-disciplinary approaches and methods helps us towards a finer appreciation of dress as "the complication of social life made visible." It would be good to be able to conclude here that all of this is now fully appreciated and that any remaining divisions between object-centered researchers and the academic world have crumbled away. There is still, however, too little formalized academic cooperation between fashion history specialists in museums and universities, certainly in Britain. There is indeed cooperation over exhibitions, visiting lectures and conferences, but when it comes to serious levels of postgraduate supervision and external examining, museum dress curators still remain largely excluded.

We, who share a driving interest in these dynamic new approaches to the history, theory and contemporary practice of fashion are collectively in a position to see off any such remaining subject- and gender-based prejudices and practices. I look forward to it.

Notes

1. Polly Binder was the author's mother. In 1939, Binder put together a picture diary of sketches in pen and colored inks of the entire process of the development and presentation of this series. She presented this to Mary Adams as a souvenir of the programmes. Sketches are reproduced here with special thanks to Sally Adams.
2. The origins of dress history could be dated to early publications such as Ferdinando Bertelli, 1556, *Omnium fere gentium habitus nostrae aetatis,* Venice; François Deszerpzs, 1564, *Recueil de la diversité des habits qui sont de présent usage,* Paris; and Jost Amman, 1577, *Habitus Praecipuorum Populorum tam Virorum quam Feminarum Singulari Arte Depicti,* Nuremberg.
3. With thanks to Amy de la Haye, Curator of Twentieth-Century Dress at the Victoria and Albert Museum, for this information.
4. With thanks to Natalie Rothstein.
5. Amy de la Haye in correspondence with the author, August 1995.
6. Beatrix Le Wita, in *French Bourgeois Culture* (Cambridge University Press, 1994: 58), writes: "What a delight it is to read the pages of Balzac's 'Autres études des femmes,' in which the author describes with quite extraordinary meticulousness how it was still possible, between 1839 and 1840, to tell a female aristocrat and a woman of the bourgeoisie apart, the key being to pay attention 'to the little details.'"

References

Barnes, Ruth and Joanne B. Eicher. 1993. *Dress and Gender, Making and Meaning*. Oxford: Berg.

Bourdieu, Pierre. 1989 (reprint), *Distinction—A Social Critique of the Judgment of Taste*. London: Routledge.

Breward, Christopher. 1995. *The Culture of Fashion*. Manchester: Manchester University Press.

Brewer, John and Roy Porter. 1993. *Consumption and the World of Goods*. London: Routledge.

Bulletin de La Société de l' Histoire du Costume. 1907–9. No. 1, June. Paris: Leroy.

Buck, Anne. 1958. *Handbook for Museum Curators*. Part D, Section 3. London: The Museums Association.

——. 1991. Buying Clothes in Bedfordshire: Customers and Tradesmen, 1700–1800, in Fabrics and Fashions, Studies in the Economic and Social History of Dress. *Textile History*, 22.2 (Autumn).

——. 1996. *Clothes and the Child—A History of Children's Dress in England, 1500–1900*. Carton.

Coleman, Elizabeth Anne. 1989. *The Opulent Era, Fashions of Worth, Doucet and Pingat*. New York and London: The Brooklyn Museum with Thames and Hudson.

Cordwell, Justine and Ronald A. Schwarz. 1979. *The Fabrics of Society, The Anthropology of Clothing and Adornment*. The Hague: Mouton.

Craik, Jennifer. 1994. *The Face of Fashion—Cultural Studies in Fashion*. London: Routledge.

Druesdow, Jean. 1987. *In Style, Celebrating Fifty Years of the Costume Institute*. New York: Metropolitan Museum of Art.

Eicher, Joanne B. 1995. *Dress and Ethnicity*. Oxford: Berg.

Evans, Caroline. 1997. "Street Style," *Costume*, 31: 105–10.

—— and Minna Thornton. 1989. *Women and Fashion, A New Look*. London: Quartet.

Fine, Ben and Ellen Leopold. 1993. *The World of Consumption*. London: Routledge.

Gibbs-Smith, Charles. 1976. "Obituary for James Laver." *Costume*, 10.

Ginsburg, Madelaine. 1962. *A Brief Guide to the Costume Court*. London: Victoria and Albert Museum.

Guillaume, Valerie. 1993. *Jacques Fath*. Paris: Paris-Musées.

Hamer, Louise. 1984. "The Cullercoats Fishwife." *Costume*, 18: 66–73.

Harrods Ltd. (no date). *Old English Costumes selected from the collection formed by Mr Talbot Hughes, a sequence of fashions through the 18th and 19th centuries, presented to the Victoria and Albert Museum, South Kensington*. London: Harrods Ltd.

Hart, Chrystal. 1980. "Bibliography of Anne Buck's Publications." *Costume*, 14: 3–5.

Harte, Negley. 1976. Book review. *Textile History*, 7: 198.

——. 1977. Review of dress history books. *Textile History*, 8: 183.

——. 1991. *The Economics of Clothing in the Late Seventeenth Century, Textile History*, 22. 2: 277.

Harte, Negley B. and Kenneth G. Ponting, eds. 1973. *Textile and Economic History: Essays in Honour of Miss Julia de Lacy Mann.*

Harvey, John. 1995. *Men in Black*. London: Reaktion.

Kopytoff, Igor. 1986. "The Cultural Biography of Things: Commoditization as Process." In *The Social Life of Things: Commodities in Cultural Perspective*, ed. Arjun Appadurai. Cambridge: Cambridge University Press.

Lansdell, Avril. 1973. *Costume In a Local History Museum: Weybridge Museum, Surrey, Costume,* 7.

Lemire, Beverly. 1991. *Fashion's Favourite—The Cotton Trade and the Consumer in Britain, 1660–1800*. Oxford: Oxford University Press.

——. 1997. *Dress, Culture and Commerce: The English Clothing Trade before the Factory, 1660–1800*. Basingstoke: Macmillan.

Levitt, Sarah. 1986. *Victorians Unbuttoned, Registered Designs for Clothing, Their Makers and Wearers*. London: Allen and Unwin.

Le Wita, Beatrix. 1994. *French Bourgeois Culture*. Cambridge: Cambridge University Press.

McCracken, Grant. 1988. *Culture and Consumption: New Approaches to the Symbolic Character of Consumption*. Bloomington, IN: Indiana University Press.

Maynard, Margaret. 1994. *Fashioned from Penury: Dress as Cultural Practice in Colonial Australia*. Cambridge: Cambridge University Press.

Miller, Daniel. 1987. *Material Culture and Mass Consumption*. Oxford: Blackwell.

——. 1995. *Acknowledging Consumption: A Review of New Studies*. London: Routledge.

——. 1995. "Consumption and Commodities." *Review of Anthropology*, 24: 143 and 157.

Morris, William. 1986 (reprint). *News From Nowhere and Selected Writings and Designs*. Harmondsworth: Penguin.

Palmer, Alexandra. 1994. "The Myth and Reality of Haute Couture, Consumption, Social Function and Style in Toronto, 1945–63." Ph.D. thesis, University of Brighton.

——. 1997. "New Directions: Fashion History Studies and Research in North America and England." *Fashion Theory*, 1/3: 297–312.

Paris-Musées/Musée de la Mode et du Costume. 1990. *Femmes Fin de Siècle, 1885–1895*. Paris: Paris-Musées.

Reddy, William M. 1984. *The Rise of Market Culture: The Textile Trade and French Society, 1750–1900*. Cambridge: Cambridge University Press.

Rexford, Nancy. 1988. "Studying Garments for Their Own Sake: Mapping the World of Costume Scholarship." Dress, 4.

Roth, Michael. 1991. *Das Kunstwerk des Monats*, Bulletin 146. Ulm: Ulmer Museum.

Rothstein, Natalie. 1990. *Silk Designs of the Eighteenth Century in the Collection of the Victoria and Albert Museum*. London: HMSO.

Rush Meyrick, Samuel and Charles Hamilton-Smith. 1815. *Costume of the Original Inhabitants of the British Islands from the Earliest Periods to the Sixth Century*. London: Thomas M'Lean.

Schreier, Barbara. 1994. *Becoming American: Clothing and the Jewish Experience, 1880–1920*. Chicago: Chicago Historical Society.

Schwarz, R. A. 1979. "Uncovering the Secret Vice: Towards an Anthropology of Clothing and Adornment." In *The Fabrics of Society: The Anthropology of Clothing and Adornment*, ed. J. M. Cordwell and R. A. Schwarz. The Hague: Mouton.

Smart Martin, Anne. 1993. "Makers, Buyers and Users—Consumerism as a Material Culture Framework," *Winterthur Portfolio*, 28 (2–4) (Summer/Autumn): 141–57.

Spufford, Margaret. 1984. *The Great Reclothing of Rural England: Petty Chapmen and Their Wares in the Seventeenth Century*. London: Hambledon Press.

Tarrant, Naomi. 1994. *The Development of Costume*. London: Routledge.

Thirsk, Joan. 1973. "The Fantastical Folly of Fashion: The English Stocking Knitting Industry 1500–1700." In *Textile and Economic History: Essays in Honour of Miss Julia de Lacy Mann*, ed. Negley B. Harte and Kenneth G. Ponting, p. 50.

Tozer, Jane. 1986. "Cunnington's Interpretation of Dress." *Costume*, 20: 16.

Vickery, Amanda. 1993. "Women and the World of Goods: A Lancashire Consumer and Her Possessions, 1751–81." In *Consumption and the World of Goods*, ed. John Brewer and Roy Porter, p. 278. London: Routledge.

Wardle, Patricia. 1997. "Divers Necessaries for his Majesty's Use and Service: Seamstresses to the Stuart Kings." *Costume*. 31: 16–27.

Weiner, Annette B. and Jane Schneider. 1989. *Cloth and Human Experience*. Washington, DC: Smithsonian Institution.

Wolfe, Tom. 1968. "The Secret Vice." In *The Kandy-colored Tangerine-flake Streamline Baby*, pp. 254–61. New York: Farrar, Straus & Giroux.

Fashion Theory, Volume 2, Issue 4, pp.359–382
Reprints available directly from the Publishers.
Photocopying permitted by licence only.
© 1998 Berg. Printed in the United Kingdom.

"Out of Many, One People": The Relativity of Dress, Race and Ethnicity to Jamaica, 1880–1907

Carol Tulloch

Carol Tulloch is a part-time lecturer
in visual culture at Middlesex
University. She has contributed
essays to *Chic Thrills* (1993), *One-
Off* (1997) and *things*. Forthcoming
work includes: a single-author
book, *The Birth of Cool: The
Culture of Dress in the Black
Diaspora*, (Berg); editorial advisor
to *A Companion to Contemporary
Black British Culture* (Routledge);
essays for *Defining Dress*
(Manchester University Press) and
The Culture of Sewing (Berg).

"Much progress depends on a kind of serendipity: it may be possible to suggest that those who are the first to reach Serendip are those who have systematically planned their journey."

Francis Celoria, *Subjects and Methods*

Introduction

"Out of Many, One People" was the new motto chosen by a government committee to appear on the three-hundred-year-old Jamaican coat-ofarms on the occasion of the island's independence from British colonial rule in 1962. The motto remains in place today. The maxim acknowledged that, in spite of Jamaica's racially heterogeneous and colonial past, a homogeneous independent nation had emerged, harmoniously united. This title was one of three I considered for a research project on the dress of working- and middle-class black, white and Indian women living in the British colony of Jamaica between 1880 and 1907. My indecision was a reflection of the complexity of the subject and the difficulties I faced in undertaking research where resources were couched in imperial discourse and severely lacked an established theoretical framework to unpack them.

This article is concerned with a reappraisal of dress history and its associated methodology. My aim is to ascertain the impact that race and ethnicity have on dress, and the methodological implications of this encounter. I argue that there is a need to return to the mechanics of dress history and meditate on its strengths and weaknesses, particularly in the study of colonial dress.

Dress is a means of "voice-consciousness" (Spivak 1995: 27). It allows the "other"—that is, colonial subjects "who are marginalized by imperial discourse [and] identified by their difference from the centre [the empire]" (Ashcroft, Griffiths and Tiffin 1998: 170)—to speak. When artfully worn, dress becomes the most resonant sign language; it can be a disturbingly powerful resource combating hegemonic discourse, and can create its own discourse based on commonalities such as race and ethnicity. I argue, therefore, that it is essential to graft the current theoretical debates that have problematized the question of race and ethnicity on to dress history. The relationship between dress and ethnicity has been adroitly discussed in such works as *Dress and Ethnicity* (Eicher: 1995) and *"New Raiments of Self": African American Clothing in the Antebellum South* (Bradley Foster: 1997). However, these works have focused on the issues separately—race and dress, ethnicity and dress.

My aim is to conjoin race and ethnicity as an indivisible agent integral to dress history. The article reviews the rationale behind the empirical and theoretical framework I constructed for my research.

Dress History Reappraised

The historiography of dress history is predominantly Eurocentric, with notable concentration on Britain and Paris.[1] Like its fellow sub-discipline, design history, published works have mainly concentrated on the "heroes" of dress or design—again European-based and white. Race has rarely impacted on dress history. John A. Walker has noted that race, though relevant to the discipline of design history, and by association dress history, has received far too little attention (Walker 1989: 19). He disputes the notion that "a nation's essence is the culture of one homogeneous race of people" because, as he notes, "most countries have a mixture of races, regions, languages and cultures." Therefore, "the concept of nation is a historical, ideological and political construct, a construct moreover which is subject to constant revision and which is the site of continual struggle between different factions within the nation-state" (1989: 119).

My research was conducted within the discipline of design history, which has the scope to tackle the issue of identity formation in a culture because it enables power relationships, gender and communication issues and their associations with objects to be deciphered. Penny Sparke suggests an approach based on "colligation," the assemblage of different historical events to produce a "single process" (Sparke 1986). Design reflects the value systems within any given society (Sparke 1986: 207). Adrian Forty states that the primary method of classifying dress in "costume history" is through sex, owing to the instant recognition of sexual difference; class, age and race offer other modes of classification (Forty 1989: 63). And that is the essence of dress history.

To study dress, whether its production, consumption or use, is to engage with objects that touch a body, an individual, a group, a society and a culture—physically, visually and psychologically. How, where and why people wear clothes are affected, inevitably, by external socio-cultural issues and events that cannot be denied. Within the context of Jamaica between 1880 and 1907, the interrelated issues of skin color and social class, race and ethnicity, group and colonial identity, colonialism and imperialism were signifiers sub-dividing the Jamaican community. Thus "alternative" groups and subcultures offer an insight into different values, and clothes can reference such values, whether custom-made or appropriated (Sparke 1986: 207). The employment of a systematically planned method to unravel the multiplicity of meanings associated with dress requires a combination of facts and theory, since "theories direct researchers to facts and give meaning and relevance to facts" (Sanders 1976: 4).

A New Avenue of Inquiry

The study of colonial dress is in its infancy. Helen Callaway (1993), Margaret Maynard (1994), and Kadiatu Kanneh (1995) have focused on colonial and post-colonial issues to situate and apply dress history and theory to the occurrences of self-representation and visibility on the bodies of indigenous "others." Maynard's extensive analysis of "dress as cultural practice in colonial Australia" frees dress studies from the archaic belief that it is merely something that "women do" and overturns the notion that it is "simplistic and summary, showing little sign of grappling with the intrinsic issues of the subject itself" (Maynard 1994: 3–5). Maynard suggests that the discipline's bid for full academic credibility can be achieved through a combination of theoretical and material investigation. Maynard notes that the study of dress is riddled with internal and external complexities and influences: "Dress, as a form of inscription, operates at the level of the body, constructing differences which produce the social body as a textured object with multi-dimensional layers, touched by the rich weave of history and culture" (Maynard 1994: 3).

Specific references to colonial dress in Jamaica are limited. In "Advertisements for Clothes in Kingston 1897–1914," Glory Robertson lists her findings, sourced from the clothing advertisements in the December issues of *The Daily Gleaner, Gall's News Letter* and *Daily Telegraph* (Robertson 1987–8). In "Pictorial Sources for Nineteenth Century Women's History: Dress as a Mirror of Attitudes to Women," Robertson considers dress as a hindrance to women's freedom. The evocative photographic evidence presented is mainly of white women in fashionable Victorian dress, and details the aesthetics of the garments, the cut of the clothing, and the wearing of trousers. The development of particular styles is considered from the European perspective in order to demonstrate the development of dress in Europe and tell the story of dress worn by middle-class Jamaican women. According to Robertson, the working class did adopt fine, not fashionable dress, worn primarily for special occasions such as weddings (Robertson: 1995).[2]

Patrick Bryan provides a short description of dress in *The Jamaican People 1880–1902*. He suggests this was a formative period based on consent and co-optation, not simply force. A key area of consideration for Bryan is speech and its reflection of Jamaica's ethnic and historical complexity; that is, the emulation of Englishness and its juxtaposition with the retention of folklore amongst the black Jamaicans. Black people who spoke good English indicated their understanding of "British culture." The language of the masses was associated with Jamaican folklore, and folkloric genres (poetry, religion, storytelling and songs) were categorized as quaint—though an indication of working-class origins. In this way indigenous Jamaican culture was accepted alongside British culture, which was actively promoted and practiced, primarily amongst the middle class (Bryan 1991: 84).

Clothes provided the same demarcation for Bryan. He presents a sketch of the dress styles adopted in Jamaica, with only a minute reference to women's dress, but intense focus on the differences between male leisure and occupational dress. Bryan reports briefly on the presence of "ethnic" dress worn by Indian and Chinese men and Syrian women in "colorful dresses like gypsies." The dress of the female elite indicated a leisured lifestyle due to the "stiff corsets, high-necked blouses, long sleeves and dresses falling over the ankles" (Bryan 1991: 85). "Working women" had two categories of clothing, "working clothes" and "Sunday best," and were clearly aware that fine clothes made a lady. There is no reference to Indian women's dress. Bryan provides no descriptive detail of "Sunday" or fashionable dress worn by black women of any class. He also fails to relate dress to race or ethnic differences, as he does when connecting speech with race (Bryan 1991: 84–5).

Robertson and Bryan have opened a window on to the subject of women's dress in Jamaica. Bryan has provided an in-depth study of the social and cultural character of Jamaica and the power relationships between the black masses and the white oligarchy. His work inspires one to consider if, and how, this relationship manifested itself in a visual, tangible form that also evoked place. Yet in these works the lack of critical analysis and contextualization of women's dress within the social and cultural history of Jamaica elides issues of race and gender in that history, and perpetuates the marginalization of dress and women.

As Simple as Black and White

The wider body of research profiles the aesthetic and communicative contributions made by dress to the social and cultural character of the island. My decision to study groups within a colonial context demonstrates that dress history can reveal much about identity formation in a culture, as well as power conflict and subversion from both national and international perspectives. The incidence of creative exchange, hybridization and co-optation amongst and between the women to produce a "manufactured self," or a reconstructed and adapted identity fashioned out of raw materials as well as a distinct form of styling, are reflected in dress choices. I hoped to make an exploratory stab at defining Jamaican dress during the period of study. In order to develop my analysis, I drew on current debates amongst sociologists and historians such as Paul Gilroy and Catherine Hall, as well as on cultural and post-colonial studies, which have addressed the concepts of race and ethnicity, plus cultural and group identity.

Paul Gilroy has addressed extensively the histories and political culture of Britain's black citizens. He has noted the presence and relevance of double-consciousness amongst black Britons, or the difficulty of being black and British simultaneously, which creates the ambivalence of either/orism: "if you are not one thing you are another, when actually you are all different things at once. It's a question of being able to inhabit them all into a framework without it being a problem."[3] He attributes this concept of the double-consciousness to "the stress of facing two ways at once" (Gilroy 1995: 1–3), or to the merging of black and white cultures:

> two great cultural assemblages, both of which have mutated through the course of the modern world that formed them and assumed new configurations. At present, they remain locked symbiotically in an antagonistic relationship marked out by the

symbolism of colors which adds to the conspicuous cultural power of their central Manichean dynamic—black and white. These colors support a special rhetoric that has grown to be associated with a language of nationality and national belonging as well as the languages of "race" and ethnic identity (Gilroy 1995: 1–2).

Gilroy has expanded this definition of what he prefers to term "black English" ethnicity to illuminate emotions associated with the competing ethnicities within the confined space of multicultural Britain. He references the importance of "cultural insiderism" (Gilroy 1995: 3), which promotes ethnic difference, group demarcation, cultural kinship and conversely national belonging and identity. Gilroy's proposals connect well with Catherine Hall's exploration into the definition of Englishness as ethnicity.

Hall focuses on the period 1834–65. She maintains that the English middle class consciously groomed itself as a distinct ethnic group not on the basis of "racially specific categories," but "in terms of cultural identity . . . [that] signified an identification with an imagined community . . . For Englishness is built on a series of assumptions about 'others' which define the nature of Englishness itself" (Hall 1995: 25–6). This, Hall believes, was a catalyst for the power conflict between the Caribbean and Britain—black and white—and shaped the emergent associated meanings of their respective identities:

> For in the struggles which took place over the definitions of empire in the nineteenth century, English men and women were constructing identities which drew on, challenged and constituted hierarchies of power formed through the axes of gender, race and class. As Stuart Hall has noted, the double legacy of slavery and emancipation still shapes what Britain meant in the Caribbean and what Caribbean means here. Until we understand that history, the ways we (meaning the British) were implicated then, the strategies we were pursuing for us as well as for them, we have little chance of constructing identities now which recognize and welcome difference, but will persist in constructing "others" as the exotic, the barbaric, those who cannot quite manage to be like "us" (Hall 1995: 33).

Jamaica between 1880 and 1907 was a multi-layered society of competing ethnicities, as it had been ever since the fifteenth century, when it came under Spanish rule and a small but dominant minority capitalized on the island's opportunities by subordinating the native population. This policy continued after 1660 when Jamaica passed into the hands of the British. The enslavement of Africans to work on predominately British-owned sugar plantations resulted in a distinct and ambivalent cultural dynamic between slaves and their British owners.

The continuous power struggle between them accelerated after emancipation in 1834, culminating in the Morant Bay Rebellion of 1865 and the introduction of a crown colony government the following year. The rebellion effectively marked the end of an era, what Clinton V. Black called the "dark ages" (Black 1994: 135). The year 1866, which witnessed accelerated reconstruction in all civic and cultural spheres, has been earmarked as the formation of modern Jamaica. Contemporary observers viewed 1880 to 1907 as a golden era of Jamaica's history, owing to the commitment by the oligarchy and the crown colony government to the reconstruction and modernization of the island, and particularly the metropolis, Kingston, which was shattered by an earthquake in 1907.

The island's history is dominated by the equivocal and turbulent relationship between British and African descendants both during and after slavery. In reality Jamaica was (and remains) a polyglot island with descendants of people from all over Europe, Africa, America, China and Syria. The largest groups were blacks, whites and Indians.[4] Colonial Jamaica, then, was a land inhabited by people who originated from other countries voluntarily or by force and retained fragments of their ethnic culture. Thus Jamaica during the period of consideration can be defined as an island of counter-cultural ethnic and subcultural groups that developed and competed under the British Imperial gaze, a hegemony meted out by the crown colony government. A key consideration of my research was the presence and the psychological importance of double-consciousness and identity amongst the inhabitants of polyglot Jamaica. This subliminal tapestry of cross-cultural reference and allegiance is perhaps best summarized by J. H. Reid's observation of the Anglo-Jamaican:

> The Jamaican white man has his peculiarities as well as man everywhere under the influence of climate, local needs, blessings, thought and feeling . . . At once he is the least Jamaican of everything pertaining to the country. He longs to return to England, if he is a native Englishman and if he is not, he thinks at least he ought to visit that country; and he speaks of it as "home" even when he has never visited it (Bryan 1991: 69).

Serendip

In combining these theoretical and historical references with the time-frame of 1880–1907, I had situated myself in the complex terrain of post-colonial studies, with dress history as a discipline, and an eye on the black British experience in the latter half of the twentieth century. My personal experience of double-consciousness, of being black and

Figure 1
East Indian girls in Jamaican
Dress, Port Antonio, 1897.
Courtesy of the National
Library of Jamaica, Kingston.

British, influenced my approach to late nineteenth- and early twentieth-century Jamaica, as I was aware of the long and unequal relationship between Britain and the island, between the British and black Jamaicans. Hence my original working title for the dissertation was "The Best of Both Worlds: Women's Dress in Jamaica 1880–1907." I wanted to compare the dress styles of black and white women in Jamaica with that worn by white women in Britain, as I then believed the power of patriarchal Britain over these groups was a good basis on which to consider their relationship. But a thesis such as this would only perpetuate negativity. The colonized woman and her dress would have been pushed further into the shadow of the British Empire, without room to discuss her culture of dress and self-image on her own terms. As I embarked on my research, I retained the title but concentrated on black, white and colored women in Jamaica.

Figure 2
This photograph of "Mrs Tyrell" formed part of an anonymous photograph album. There is no indication as to when the photograph was taken, but analysis of her dress reveals a mix of period styles. The drapes, pleats and folds, the subtle edging and defined waist, along with the protruding bustle are details in line with the mid-1880s. The long sleeves are a feature of the late 1870s and her hairstyle is dated as c.1874–5. Courtesy of the Jamaica Archives, Spanish Town.

The empirical research conducted in Jamaica changed my orientation completely and produced a second working title, "Out of Many One People?" Travel guides and books revealed how British and American writers viewed Jamaica and its inhabitants. The black peasantry and Indian women were very visible in such works, whilst the black, white and colored middle class were effectively invisible. Photographs disclosed that Indian women were sharing the dress styles and accessories of other ethnic groups, and that white middle-class women had constructed hybridized garments that reflected the aesthetics of their personal image.[5]

Most significantly, this leg of the research led me to consider late nineteenth-century black Jamaican women as African-Jamaican, a term I had not encountered during my research. Such an epithet is important in establishing black Jamaicans historically as being different from their black British descendants, and gives a pronounced definition and authenticity to the issue of "[dis]continuity" in the lineage and cultural identity of African slaves, black Jamaicans and black Britons of Jamaican descent. African-Jamaican women had reconstructed themselves, following emancipation. This was perhaps not a great movement globally, but on a national and local scale, and seen through the eyes of a dress historian, the shift in attitude to, and adoption of, a hybridized or fashionable dress by African-Jamaican women represented a significant assertion of cultural autonomy. As Stuart Hall notes: "This is an exciting period . . . [where] a distinct Jamaican style was beginning to emerge."[6] The dress styles worn by women in Jamaica reflected this assertion of identity, which can only be fully revealed in a comparative context— hence my emphasis on the dress culture of the other major groups of white and Indian women who enjoyed a similar experience. These female groups were exposed to each other under powerful colonial and imperial forces that naturally created a cultural and social distance, and inevitably fragmentation. The study of the dress worn by representatives of these groups bridged this divide on an aesthetic level with innocent objects such as fabric for a dress or headtie.

Ultimately I decided that the most appropriate title for my research was "Fashioned In Black and White: Women's Dress in Jamaica 1880– 1907." This, for me, summarized the critique taken on the historical myths and perceptions of women's dress in the British colony of Jamaica. The relationship between Jamaica and Britain, between black and white from 1880 to 1907, was not as simple as "black and white," but, paradoxically, it was as complex as black and white.

Race and Ethnicity

Unquestionably, race is in the foreground of my work. Race, in this narrative, informs the historiography, the rhetoric and the "material effect" of imperial discourse and at once renders the host body, and most notably a female body, visibly invisible, "even more deeply in shadow" (Spivak 1995: 28). My use of the term African-Jamaican, for example, and the inclusion of the hyphen, references the link between the racial legacy and historiography of this socially and culturally historical phenomenon. The term acknowledges African-Jamaicans' racial origins in Africa, but equally acknowledges a shift in racial "categorization" towards a blend of two cultures, two societies. The identity of late nineteenth-century African-Jamaicans, like that of African-Americans and the Black-British in the late twentieth century, was "constructed along racial as well as ethnic lines" (Ashcroft *et al.* 1998: 84).

The construct of ethnicity, whilst inextricably linked with race, offers the dress historian an additional dimension. It allows for interdisciplinary investigation across races. Consequently, my research aimed to uncover the self-presentation practiced under the shadow of imperialism and colonialism by African-Jamaican, white colonial, white-Jamaican, Indian and Indian-Jamaican women. The imperial discourse of the late nineteenth century can still wreak havoc in the late twentieth century. In the archives of Europe, and in my case Britain, the diaries and travel guides, the photographs, postcards and novels produced by British and American travellers, settlers and photographers, as well as white Jamaican photographers, entrepreneurs and merchants, are predominantly couched in imperial "truth" for future historians to confront. These were also to be found in Jamaica. The list extended to include journals, letter books and family albums.

It was therefore imperative that I consider the "other" voices when researching the archives of British imperialistic views of another country. The question is, when dealing with an "overseas history" (Wesseling: 1991) whilst based in Britain, how does the design historian find the voice of the "other"? It was on the island of Jamaica, not Britain, that the voices of African-Jamaicans and Indians were to be found: in documentary photographs of African-Jamaican and Indian working-class and peasant women; in newspapers[7] aimed specifically at the black community; and in the rich vein of evocative and detailed data stored in the *Jamaican Memories,* a collection of essays produced in response to a competition held by the Jamaican newspaper, *The Daily Gleaner,* in 1959. The latter competition was open to people over sixty years of age who were asked to recall their memories in a maximum of 1,800 words. Entries came from all over the island, Canada and Britain and included males and females from different classes, the illiterate (who dictated to their grandchildren), retired schoolteachers, sailors, the peasantry, and the middle class. Had I neglected to investigate this source, I would have continued the legacy of disallowing these other "truths" to be heard.

The material evidence I uncovered in the British and Jamaican archives with regard to the culture of dress was divided into four categories: production, consumption, use and representation. As there are no public dress collections for these women during this period, photography was central to the visualization of them. The photograph as object acts as an incubator of history. Each "reading," depending on the period, place and context, allows for new interpretations and gives birth to new meanings. This flexibility of the photograph to change with time whilst remaining "the eye of history" (Samuel 1994) is due to "The power of these pictures . . We may think we are going to them for knowledge about the past, but it is the knowledge we bring to them which makes them historically significant, transforming a more or less chance residue of the past into a precious icon" (Samuel 1994: 328). The debates surrounding the validity of photography as a valid "peg for authorial commentary" can be expanded to incorporate all the resources employed as new ways of interpreting history (Stafford 1994; Samuel 1994; Bate

1993): "We must frame a unified theory of imaging through the intersections of the old historical arts [and text] with the new optical technologies . . . for not receiving pictures [or any resource] passively but for entering and reassembling them actively" (Stafford 1994: 473).

I constructed from postcards, documentary photography and family albums a series of *tableaux vivants*[8] of black, white and Indian women—the indigenous people and the indentured immigrants, tourists and "settlers"[9]—to provide evidence of their existence and consequently their dress styles. Photographic evidence can be problematic, however: were the clothes worn in the photographs borrowed? was the photograph art direct? was the subject styled by another individual with a particular form of representation in mind? who took the photograph? These pieces of vital evidence, which have impact on the level of "voice" the image can attribute to the wearer and consequently the ethnic group, all merit inquiry. Nonetheless, the value of photographs is clear: simultaneously the historically silent voices of black, white and Indian women could "speak" through dress. In developing my methodology, I consciously planned to find the voice of the "other," to reveal an alternative "truth" to the representation of black, white and Indian women in Jamaica that had been disseminated through imperialist discourse.[10]

The impact of race and ethnicity on dress in combination with dress history's ability to give "voices" to silenced peoples should serve as an incentive for the discipline to contribute to the current academic spotlight on "other" histories. Dress history has the methodological facility to reassess the representation and subjectivity of colonized subjects in relation to the colonizer. Much of the current historiography maintains the hegemony of the latter and was informed by imperial tracts, such as novels, travel guides, postcards and photographs. The re-evaluation of received history is an ambitious and complicated task, but may overturn misconceptions. Post-colonial concerns relating to race and ethnicity, the "other" and subjectivity, imperialism and the post-colonial body should not be divorced from dress history, which at times has privileged aesthetics at the expense of meaning. Dress has the unusual capacity to straddle the polarized realms of the public and the private, owing to its extended relationship with other spheres: sexuality, gender and the body (Maynard 1994: 3), which in turn connect with race and ethnicity. The triangulatory issue of "race–ethnicity–dress" can be meaningfully deployed across period, space and place.

Race–Ethnicity–Dress

The catalyst for my research was a late nineteenth-century photograph entitled "Jubilee Market Kingston, Jamaica." To find an image of black women, more specifically black women "hanging around" Jamaica's metropolis Kingston, *c.*1895, gave me a sense of connection and identity. Ludicrously, I had thought that fine dress emerged amongst black Jamaicans in the 1950s, as I had never seen examples of well-dressed black Jamaicans prior to this photograph—only anthropological photographs of partially clothed African women, and paintings and engravings of slave women, laborers, and African-American domestics in work clothes.

My interest was fired further on closer study of the photograph and the inscription on the back: "In the land of Jamaica, West Indies. Carrying their day's shopping on their heads while they stop for a chat outside the Jubilee Market Kingston, Jamaica." The caption draws the viewer's attention to a specific action of working-class practice. In the photograph, only two women carry baskets on their heads. Most of the others are well dressed in "Victorian" clothing (a detail invisible to the caption writer). "Victorian" dress has been translated as a Western, and more specifically a British style, with Paris positioned as the undisputed fashion capital of the period. Valerie Steele has stated that what we think of as Victorian fashion lasted from 1820 to *circa* 1910 and therefore correlates only loosely with the actual reign of Queen Victoria (Steele 1985: 51). This imprecision leads one to consider the wider definitions of Victorian fashion, Victorian style, Victorian dress and their cultural relativity and sense of self in relation to the British colony of Jamaica and its various female groups.

In my decision to study women's dress in late nineteenth- and early twentieth-century Jamaica, I wanted to move away from ethnic absolutism, particularly as the multicultural profile of 1990s Britain bears surface similarities to the British colony of Jamaica in the 1890s, which was, as I mentioned earlier, a point at which Jamaica attained a level of autonomy, in spite of colonial rule. Rather than concentrate on what appeared to be working-class black women featured in this photograph, I wanted to pursue the "authentic" Jamaica and thereby consider the predominant colonial subjects of black, white, and Indian groups, their relationships and the occurrence of social or cultural interface. William A. Green has argued that the dialectical methodology of perpetual struggle between African and Euro-Caribbeans, between rich and poor, and between blacks and whites is a "blunt and imperfect instrument for pursuing Caribbean history in the nineteenth century" (Green 1993: 28–9). I hoped, through the study of one photograph, "to fix the truth of the past . . . [and to] unsettle the certainty of history and render it more contestable" (Ryan 1997: 225).

The subjective approach to the study of the creolization of the West Indies brings about the "identification of people, whatever their place of origin or racial composition, with the island societies in which they lived" (Green 1993: 28). Pioneers such as Edward Braithwaite, Philip Curtin and Sidney Mintz concentrated on slave, ex-slave and laboring African-Caribbeans. For Green these approaches are insufficient, even

Figure 3
The following caption bears
little similarity to the actual
photograph dated c. 1895:
"In the Land of Jamaica W.I.
Carrying their day's shopping
on their heads while they stop
for a chat outside the Jubilee
Market, Kingston, Jamaica"
© Carol Tulloch.

when combined, if historians are to pursue the study of West Indian
integration and "specify those characteristics of the area ... that give it
particularity and commonality—to discover what is authentically
Caribbean" (Mintz 1967: 141). He encourages historians to consider
the perpetual and inescapable external forces which shaped Caribbean
society (Green 1993: 36).

Infrastructure: The Presence of the Past in the Present

> Nowhere else in the Black Diaspora did I have such a sense of the
> slave past as in Jamaica . . . For in Jamaica, along with a social
> order that seems to bear the tracks of the slave past, as fossilized
> rocks retain the prints of some extinct species in its passage, there
> is the counterculture of a consciousness that reaches back to an
> old resistance and in doing so, accepts the experience of the slave,
> not as servile but as defiant (Segal 1995: 317).

Ronald Segal suggests that the notion of the historic present shapes
the character of Jamaica. He defines Jamaica of the 1990s through a
list of cultural motifs: violence; gang membership; the polarity between
rich and poor and the powerful and the powerless, which is coded by
skin color; music and Rastafarianism (Segal 1995: 315). What of dress?
Is "Jamaican dress" unique? Does it begin v ith the Rasta Tam, which
is the woollen knitted or crocheted hat in red, gold and green, that
communicates the wearer's consciousness of the ideologies surrounding

"Blackness" and African roots? The leap is surely too great. What of the "quiet years" following emancipation in 1834? Was this really a fallow period that had no influence on Jamaica's future social and cultural character? These questions and Segal's observations of contemporary Jamaica beg one to consider the presence of the past in the present and the interrelationships of power, space, time and distance.

Thorstein Veblen's *The Theory of the Leisure Class* is central to any dress historian's analysis of the relationship between power and clothing. A work contemporary to the period under study, its usefulness for my research was authenticated by Veblen's own immigrant origins. He was born in America of Norwegian parents, and therefore lived the experience of "double identity." Veblen's treatment of consumption, display and the hereditary present is an intelligent model for the dress historian wishing to grapple with the dress worn by colonials and the colonized. He considered the concept of the hereditary present to qualify the existence of cultural traits in the leisured class, "transmitted approximately as they have stood in the recent past" (Veblen 1970[1899]: 147).

Veblen's argument was Eurocentrically based. He considered the traits of the "two or three main ethnic types that go to make up the Occidental populations . . . hybrids of the prevailing ethnic elements combined in the most varied proportions; with the result that they tend to take back to one or the other of the component ethnic types" (Veblen 1970: 147–8). The definition of Europeans as ethnic types led Veblen to expand on the development of the leisured and dominant class—from their roots in a barbarian culture, to a predatory culture and lastly a pecuniary culture and a "master" class. Veblen cited as their "most splendid traits" (Veblen 1970: 157) the possession of wealth, a ruthlessly consistent sense of status, the typical aristocratic virtues, as well as providence, prudence and chicanery: "Life in a modern industrial community or in other words, life under a pecuniary culture, acts by a process of selection to develop and conserve a certain range of aptitudes and propensities" (Veblen 1970: 160).

Veblen's theory that Europeans were an ethnic group adds credence to the current debate on ethnicity as a European feature outlined earlier. Veblen felt all classes were to an extent "engaged in the pecuniary struggle." The lower orders, such as domestic servants, complied with the transition and retention of "aristocratic archaic traits of character." From the prescriptive position of the leisure class domestic servants learn "what is good and beautiful" and apply this knowledge in their own space. Veblen read this transference of character traits as the emergence of a new class, a large under-class, built on the archaic traits of the leisure class. However, this also implied a total negation of the ability of the under-class, regardless of their location in the world, to build a culture of their own. Furthermore, he suggested that they could not inhabit two cultures, or their own alongside the traits imposed upon them from the dominant group.

Space and Distance

Veblen's theories were directed at a Caucasian leisure class. In order to expand his ideas and incorporate a wider, ethnically mixed audience, it is useful to consider Stephen Kern's argument that every age has a distinctive sense of the past, with specific meanings for individuals, an inspiration on which to build for future personal and national development (Ken: 1983). Thus individual experience of the past is used to articulate and challenge the status quo. This can affect a wider audience, on the basis of a journey from the personal past to the homogeneous historic past. Thereby, individuals can interpret the past in different ways. The past, then, equates with time "which is heterogeneous, fluid and reversible" (Kern 1983: 64). Space, Kern argues, is also a heterogeneous "prime symbol" of culture that "varies from society to society . . . different properties in different regions" (Kern 1983: 138) and is under constant threat of usurpation and reconstruction by other cultures, each with their unique sense of space. Kern believes that the delineation of space and its extension beyond physical locations to specific cultural and social areas, such as political institutions, religious myths, ethical ideals, principles of science, and forms of painting, music, and sculpture (and I would add dress), are important in conceptualizing a particular culture, as it is necessary to accommodate ones own interpretation of man's aspects of a culture to its own particular notion of extenison. (Kern 1983: 138–9).

Kern defines geographical distance as an imperial tool that "developed along with the great expansion of empires in the late nineteenth century and was especially concerned with the way the size of states, their location, and the distances between them shaped their politics and history" (Kern 1983: 223). Conversely, geographical and cultural distance were unprecedentedly unified and intensified between 1880 and 1918. Technology, communication and transportation were mediated by urbanism and imperialism, which generated a neighborly sense of distance. The proliferation of travel data in magazines, guide books, gazetteers, maps and travel companies encouraged global travel. By 1907 the world traveller became a legitimate entity called "the globetrotter" (Kern 1983: 230).[11] The reduction of vast geographical distances between different cultures, Kern suggests, encouraged a cultural "creative interchange." The press and increased levels of literacy also brought an expansion of information at home and abroad, and enabled the public to become better informed of the cultural and political climate around the world. People were able to travel and gain knowledge of the world from the printed page and therefore "distance lost its meaning along all lines of latitude and longitude [along which] British capital worked its way" (Kern 1983: 231).[12]

Power and Relationship

The class relations in a Malay village were the inspiration for the book *Domination and the Arts of Resistance: Hidden Transcripts*, by James C. Scott: "the poor sang one tune when they were in the presence of the rich and another tune when they were among the poor [the 'public transcript' and 'hidden transcript' respectively]. The rich too spoke one way to the poor and another among themselves." (Scott 1990:ix). To label what Scott suggests to be a display of pretence as "the public and hidden transcripts," the unwritten rules which the groups adhere to, is Scott's attempt to intensify the reasoning behind why the public relationship (the "public transcript") taken alone misrepresents or conceals the power relations between "subordinate and dominant groups." The discourse of this "public transcript" is undermined by the contentious co-presence of the "hidden transcript," and the resultant nervous energy that infuses the power relationships between their respective discourses.

Scott's postmodernist, ahistorical approach considers power relations within the context of verbal communication; but what of visual communication utilizing the "public and hidden transcripts" to interpret the discourse of power relations between such groups? As a supplement to Veblen, Scott offers greater insight into the interplay between dominant and subordinate groups, and the spaces they inhabit. Scott's explanation of the elite group's method of creating social distance from their "inferiors" is parallel to Veblen's use of fashionable dress, consumption and etiquette. The social space inhabited by the lower order is shaped by a dense social interaction among subordinates and very restricted, formal contact with superiors that fosters the growth of distinctive subcultures and the diverging dialects that accompany them (Scott 1990: 133–4). This leads to a structural kinship that develops in communities, such as slave communities, where a critique of domination is shared.

Scott identified two divisions of the subordinate group. The first is a cohesive, interdependent community where all aspects of social life—work, community, authority and leisure—serve to maximize the cohesion and unity of the subculture, as in the rural peasantry of Jamaica. The second is more heterogeneous. Its people live in mixed neighborhoods and work at different jobs, and their interests and social focus are more dispersed and diverse (Scott 1990: 135). Both develop their own "dialect," which I propose can be expressed not only through speech, but through specific styles of dress, as well as codes, myths, shared heroes and social standards, to constitute a distinctive subculture. The development of subcultures (which Scott suggests have been present since the Middle Ages), and the sharpening of hidden transcripts, emerge in tandem within public terrains such as the marketplace, where unmediated versions of the hidden transcript can be encountered. Scott warns

that even amongst an apparently tenacious subculture, some do break
ranks and emulate the dominant group (Scott 1990: 130).

Postmodernism

The fragmented and complex composition of Jamaica requires a method
of interpreting the imagery of the period. This consists of the elements
that Angela McRobbie equates with postmodernism, an endless cross-
referencing of images, a pastiche on reality (McRobbie 1995). Elizabeth
Wilson views postmodernism as an enveloping condition, a portmanteau
category that aestheticizes dystopia and the fragmentation of knowledge
and identities (Wilson 1992: 4–7). In applying postmodernist theory to
Jamaica in the 1890s, I tried to understand the formation of a new society
that replaced the old world where the majority of the inhabitants were
enslaved—a society that made use of the old and the new and the past
in the present by juxtaposing imageries, spaces and ideologies. Jamaicans
were not following a predominant tradition all of their own, but
retaining and borrowing the traits, traditions and motifs from English,
Scottish, African, Indian, German, French and Jewish sources created
outside the island that all informed the popular culture of the period.
Wilson states:

> . . . in a fragmenting world others feel that they can in some way
> "choose" the identity they were born with, or redefine and rework
> it. Yet ultimately we do not choose our bodies, so postmodern
> playfulness can never entirely win the day . . . Dress could play a
> part, for example, either to glue the false identity together on the
> surface, or to lend a theatrical and play-acting aspect to the
> hallucinatory experience of the contemporary world; we become
> actors, inventing our costumes for each successive appearance,
> disguising the recalcitrant body we can never entirely transform.
> Perhaps style becomes a substitute for identity, perhaps its fluidity
> (in theory it can be changed at will) offers an alternative to the
> stagnant fixity of "old-fashioned" ideas of personality and core
> identity (moving way from the subordinate image) perhaps on the
> contrary it is used to fix identity more firmly. Either way, we may
> still understand dress as one tool in the creation of identities
> (Wilson 1992: 8–9).

Postmodernist theory allows us to acknowledge fragmentation, "the
split between thought and feeling," that occurs between and amongst
the dominant and subordinate groups, and their expression of the space
they share in all spheres of cultural life, as well as the occurrence of
engagement and collision, which in turn becomes part of the hidden and
public transcripts. Should the style of dress mirror the social order, then
it has materialized into the hidden transcript of the particular group,

and "reinforced class barriers and other forms of difference" (Wilson 1992: 9).

The Rhetoric of Imperialism

Britain had an equivocal perception of Jamaica and its subjects. The romantic view was directed at the natural beauty of "their" island, what can be described as an extension of the British countryside, and affectionately known as "Our Island of Springs." From the late 1880s, there was a concentrated effort by the middle-class merchants on the island to establish and develop a tourist industry in Jamaica. Prior to the 1890s, visitors were wooed to Jamaica as potential settlers or investors. A number of factors affected the development of a tourist industry, including excellent shipping connections with Europe and America, eradication of diseases such as yellow fever and malaria, an established system of railway lines to the larger towns, a telegraph and telephone system, underground waste disposal systems, a cheap tramcar service from the city to the boundaries, and electricity and piped water in the larger towns and the city of Kingston.

Tourism, like fashion, has the ability "to reveal normal practices which might otherwise remain opaque" (Urry 1990: 2). To consider how social groups construct their tourist gaze is a means of investigating what is happening in "normal society." The concept of difference can be used to locate the normal through an inquiry into the typical forms of tourism (Urry 1990: 2).

Urry believes there is no single tourist gaze. Rather, the tourist gaze is dependent on society and historical period. Such gazes are constructed through difference, socially organized and systematized. Urry explains that there are professional experts who help to construct and develop the tourist gaze. What expertise did nineteenth-century male and female travel writers who provided prospective tourists to Jamaica have, other than their social class and nationality? How did their gaze relate and respond to the Jamaican women in terms of class, race and ethnicity? The answers to such questions relate directly to the tourists' descriptions of the women, particularly of their dress, which were written from imperialist and misogynistic perspectives.

The relationship between African Jamaicans and their "Mother Country" was tenuous. Victorian Britain had primarily acquired knowledge and perceptions of black people from the activities of the anti-slavery movement and lecturers and writers who had visited British colonies. From the 1880s onwards, there was obsessive observation of black women in their working dress photographed as objects of study and documentary by white middle-class men, a practice that can be compared with the work conducted by Record Survey photographers of white working-class women in Britain during the mid- to late nineteenth-century. These photographs were generally taken by tourists-cum-travel writers and professional photographers and were vital resources for the burgeoning tourist industry in the form of tourist guides and the revolutionary news medium—the postcard. With hindsight, the postcard can be defined as an educational tool that featured pictorial depictions of the Empire and "ethnics showing the whole range of indigenous people under imperial rule" (MacKenzie 1984: 16). Therefore the images received in Britain of Jamaicans were a means of self-edification. In the light of this my research had to consider the visual images of the various female social groups that were presented to Victorians as "true" representations of women in Jamaica.

Britain's imperialist discourse included an eccentric perception that extended to British settlers in the Empire, who were characterized as "going native." Though this group constituted a colony's elite, Britain viewed them as having "degenerated" owing to prolonged contact with the indigenous culture, regardless of its degree, and as a consequence they were deemed inferior to their British equivalents (Ashcroft, Griffiths and Tiffin 1998: 47–8, 115).

This framework provided me with specific aims: to explain how dress worn by women in Jamaica between 1880 and 1907 was shaped by the events of the past and was informed by those experiences during the period of study; to consider how dress materialized the unwritten "hidden and public transcripts" adopted by the variant ethnic groups; to examine how the relationships between Jamaica's dominant and subordinate groups may have been marked by those who possessed or were denied power; and finally, in turn, to consider how this affected the social and cultural space the groups occupied and thereby influenced their respective dress styles.

Conclusion

The problems I faced at the outset of the research were compounded by my subject's complexities and the absence of an established academic framework within which to examine them. What were the aesthetic and communicative contributions made by the production, the consumption and use of dress to the social and cultural character of the British colony of Jamaica? In presenting a sense of place and the definitive flavor of Jamaican women's dress during this period, irrespective of class and ethnicity, the study went beyond the boundaries of design history and straddled the fields of dress history and material and visual culture. Such a cross-fertilization of methodologies and skills applied to the "study of a culture at a distance" was addressed by Margaret Mead and Rhoda Metraux as early as 1953.[13]

In terms of understanding the history of dress in Jamaica and any consequential influence it may have in the latter half of the twentieth century, I was no longer seduced by late twentieth-century Britain as the starting-point of a distinct form of Jamaican dress. Rather it is the other way around: late nineteenth-century Jamaica now influences my views on how late twentieth-century black Britons create a distinctive style. Locating African-Jamaican women and their culture of dress in this period alongside that of Indian and white women in Jamaica has, I hope, gone some way to closing the gap on the history of dress culture in Jamaica. "Jamaican dress" and its associated Jamaican aesthetic style formation did not begin in Britain as part of a black counter-cultural quake after the Second War. Its roots stretched back to slavery and crystallized in the period 1880–1907. Jamaican dress was informed by the intersection of races and ethnicities. I would like to see that dress history is informed by these matters as well.

Acknowledgements

I would like to thank Sarah Levitt for her dress history expertise, and Melanie Unwin and Syd Shelton for editorial and photographic work respectively.

Notes

1. Until recently, this was also the case for museum dress collections, but institutions such as the V&A and the British Empire and Commonwealth Museum have attempted to redress this.
2. I would like to thank Glory Robertson for all her help during my research.
3. Paul Gilroy in interview with the writer, 18 September 1987.
4. The Jamaican census for 1891 states that the population, according to color, was black 488,624 (76.41%), colored 121,955 (19.07%), white 14,692 (2.29%), East Indians 10,116 (1.58%).
5. For an extended outline of this see Carol Tulloch, "Fashioned in Black and White: Women's Dress in Jamaica, 1880–1907" in *things*, 7, Winter 1997–8.
6. Stuart Hall gave this response following a presentation by the author of her MA research at the Royal College of Art, 12 December 1996.
7. Black newspapers such as the *Jamaican Advocate* are not available in Britain.
8. "*Tableau vivant*" refers to "a silent and motionless group of people arranged to represent a scene," *The Oxford English Dictionary*.
9. The term "settler," in post-colonial theory, generally refers to Europeans who move from their country of origin to their respective colony with the intention of establishing permanent residence. See Ashcroft, Griffiths and Tiffin 1998: 210.

10. The debate on the level of truth associated with imperial discourse, particularly that of Britain, has been widely documented. See Ashcroft, Griffiths and Tiffin 1998: 122–7; Ryan 1997; Said 1993; MacKenzie 1990, 1986, 1984.

11. The term "globetrotter" was cited as new jargon in a popular German travel guide of 1907, Karl Lamprecht, *Deutsche Geschichte der Jungesten Vergangenheit und gegenwart*, 1912.

12. Quotation taken from Herbert Feis in *Europe The World's Banker 1870–1914* (1965).

13. The authors believed such an approach was of paramount importance in the tracing and analysis of the "cultural character structure of members of a complex literate contemporary society," if one is to get a sense of the larger whole of the culture.

References

Ashcroft, Bill, Gareth Griffiths and Helen Tiffin, eds. 1995. *The Post-Colonial Studies Reader*. London, New York: Routledge.

——. 1998. *Key Concepts in Post-Colonial Studies*. London, New York: Routledge.

Bate, David. 1993. "Photography and the Colonial Vision" in *Third Text*. 22, Spring. London: Kala.

Black, Clinton V. 1994. *The History of Jamaica*. Harlow: Longman.

Bradley Foster, Helen. 1997. *"New Raiments of Self": African American Clothing in the Antebellum South*. Oxford: Berg.

Bryan, Robert. 1991. *The Jamaican People 1880–1902: Race, Class and Social Control*. London: Macmillan Education.

Callaway, Helen. 1993. "Dressing for Dinner in the Bush: Rituals of Self-Definition and British Imperial Authority" in *Dress and Gender*, ed. R. Barnes and J. Eicher. Oxford: Berg.

Eicher, Joanne B. 1995. *Dress and Ethnicity*. Oxford, Washington D.C.: Berg.

Forty, Adrian. 1989. *Objects of Desire: Design and Society 1750–1980*. London: Thames & Hudson.

Gilroy, Paul. 1995. *The Black Atlantic: Modernity and Double Consciousness*. London: Verso.

Green, William A. 1993. "The Creolization of Caribbean History: The Emancipation Era and a Critique of Dialectical Analysis" in *Caribbean Freedom: Economy and Society, from Emancipation to the Present* by H. Beckles and V. Shepherd. Kingston: Ian Randle; London: James Currey.

Hall, Catherine. 1995. *White, Male and Middle Class: Explorations in Feminism and History*. Cambridge: Polity Press.

Kanneh, Kadiatu. 1995. "Feminism and the Colonial Body." In *The Post-Colonial Studies Reader*, ed. B. Ashcroft, G. Griffiths and H. Tiffin. London and New York: Routledge.

Kern, Stephen. 1983. *The Culture of Time and Space, 1880–1918.* London: Weidenfeld and Nicolson.

MacKenzie, John M. 1984. *Propoganda and Empire. The Manipulation of British Public Opinion 1880–1960* Manchester, New York: Manchester University Press.

——. 1990. *Imperialism and the Natural World.* Manchester, New York: Manchester University Press.

McRobbie, Angela. 1995. *Postmodernism and Popular Culture.* London, New York: Routledge.

Maynard, Margaret. 1994. *Fashioned from Penury: Dress as Cultural Practice in Colonial Australia.* New York, Melbourne: Cambridge University Press.

Mead, Margaret and Rhoda Metraux. 1953. *The Study of Culture at a Distance.* Chicago: University of Chicago Press.

Mintz, Sidney W. 1967. "Caribbean Nationhood, an Anthropological Perspective." In *Caribbean Integration: Papers on Social, Political and Economic Integration,* ed. S. Lewis and T. G. Matthews.

Robertson, Glory. 1987–8. "Advertisements for Clothes in Kingston 1897–1914." *Jamaica Journal,* November.

——. 1995. "Pictorial Sources for Nineteenth-Century Women's History: Dress as a Mirror of Attitudes to Women" in *Engendering History: Caribbean Women in Historical Perspective,* ed. V. Shepherd, B. Brereton and B. Bailey. Kingston: Ian Randle; London: James Currey.

Ryan, James R. 1997. *Picturing Empire: Photography and the Visualization of the British Empire.* London: Reaktion Books.

Said, Edward W. 1993. *Culture and Imperialism.* London: Chatto and Windus.

Samuel, Raphael. 1994. *Theatres of Memory Vol I: Past and Present in Contemporary Culture.* London: Verso.

Sanders, William B. 1976. *The Sociologist as Detective: An Introduction to Research Methods.* New York: Praeger.

Scott, James C. 1990. *Domination and the Arts of Resistance: Hidden Transcripts.* New Haven, London: Yale University Press.

Segal, Ronald. 1995. *The Black Diaspora.* London: Faber & Faber.

Sparke, Penny. 1986. *An Introduction to Design and Culture in the Twentieth Century.* London: Allen & Unwin.

Spivak, Gayatri Chakravorty. 1995. "Can the Subaltern Speak?" in *The Post-Colonial Studies Reader,* ed. B. Ashcroft, G. Griffiths and H. Tiffin. London and New York: Routledge.

Stafford, B. M. 1994. "Presuming Images and Consuming Words: The Visualisation of Knowledge from the Enlightenment to Post-Modernism" in *Consumption and the World of Goods,* ed. J. Brewer and R. Porter. London and New York: Routledge.

Steele, Valerie. 1985. *Fashion and Eroticism: Ideals of Feminine Beauty from the Victorian Era to the Jazz Age.* New York: Oxford University Press.

Tulloch, Carol. 1997–8. "Fashioned in Black and White: Women's Dress in Jamaica, 1880–1907" in *things*, 7, Winter.

Urry, John. 1990. *The Tourist Gaze: Leisure and Travel in Contemporary Societies*. London: Sage.

Veblen, Thorstein. 1970 [1899]. *The Theory of the Leisure Class*. London: Unwin Books.

Walker, John A. 1989. *Design History and the History of Design*. London: Pluto Press.

Wesseling, H. 1991. "Overseas History." In *New Perspectives on Historical Writing*, ed. P. Burke. Cambridge: Polity Press.

Wilson, Elizabeth. 1992. "Fashion and the Postmodern Body." In *Chic Thrills: A Fashion Reader*, ed. J. Ash and E Wilson. London: Pandora.

Fashion Theory, Volume 2, Issue 4, pp.383–390
Reprints available directly from the Publishers.
Photocopying permitted by licence only.

Dress in History: Reflections on a Contested Terrain

John Styles

John Styles is Head of Postgraduate studies at the Victoria
and Albert Museum in London,
responsible for the M.A. program in
the History of Design run jointly by
the Museum and the Royal College
of Art. He has published extensively on design and manufacturing
in eighteenth-century England, with
a particular emphasis on textiles
and dress. He is currently writing a
book entitled *Clothes, Fashion and
the Plebeian Consumer in England,
1660 to 1820*.

The title of the conference that gave rise to this collection of articles
was "Dress in History." In the course of the conference a great deal was
said about dress, but rather less about history. These concluding
comments are concerned with the difficulties, conceptual and methodological, of reinserting dress into history. In addressing those difficulties
I shall reflect on the tensions between object-based and other modes of
scholarship that have dogged the history of dress and fashion. These
are tensions that are unusually potent and intractable, most obviously
because they so often reflect professional divisions between those who
study surviving garments and accessories, especially in museums, and
those who study dress through images and words, often in higher

education. In reflecting on these divisions, my aim is to move beyond issues of methodology—how we do the history of dress—and to raise the more fundamental question of why we study the history of dress.

Appropriately I shall begin with the history of the subject itself, which is dealt with so eloquently by Lou Taylor elsewhere in this volume. As she points out, for most of the last hundred and fifty years, as art museums multiplied and a host of new academic disciplines established themselves in the universities, the study of historic clothing and the history of clothing remained marginalized in these institutions. In some senses it still remains so, although the situation has changed radically since the Second World War, and particularly since the 1970s. Why have matters changed? In addressing that question I want to focus on intellectual rather than institutional issues, while not denying the force of Lou Taylor's observations about the importance of gender prejudice in explaining the widespread institutional animosity towards dress and its history.

In the first half of the twentieth century that institutional animosity was profound. As Lou Taylor's essay makes clear, insofar as museums in the period collected post-Medieval western dress at all, it was rarely with great enthusiasm. Often clothes were prized more for the textiles from which they were made than for their design and aesthetic qualities as dress. What interest there was remained largely confined to high fashion. But at least some important museums did develop collections in this period, however grudgingly. In the universities, by contrast, the history of dress featured hardly at all. Professional university historians concerned themselves overwhelmingly with the history of high politics. Economic and social history was struggling to establish a foothold within the academy. It remained firmly anchored in the history of production, especially the transformation of production wrought by factory industrialization. Economic historians wrote extensively about how clothing materials were produced, but with few exceptions their histories concluded at the textile factory gate. Clothing and its production were too fragmented, too small-scale, in a sense too primitive to incorporate into their grand narratives of industrialization. Similarly, for those economic historians (often women) who worked on social conditions and social policy, clothing was simply not important enough when set alongside grand themes like hunger or unemployment. Some academic research did grapple with fashion in these years, but it was hardly ever undertaken by historians. Such studies mainly considered fashion in its relationship to economic, sociological, or psychological theory. Most of this work was ahistorical, for instance those studies that contributed to the early development of market research, but there were exceptions, most notably J. Flugel's *Psychology of Clothes* with its historical analysis of "the great masculine renunciation".[1] Nevertheless, even at their most historical, hardly any of these academic studies can be said to have developed a sustained focus on the history of dress in its own right.

Not a great deal changed in the decades immediately after the Second World War. Interest in the history of dress at the Courtauld Institute in London arose initially because art historians were anxious to use historical knowledge of clothes to date paintings. As in the museums of the 1950s and 1960s, the incorporation of fashionable dress into the category of art history came only slowly and grudgingly. Indeed it is really only since the 1970s that the history of dress has blossomed in the academy. The reasons for this blossoming are many and various, but three important sources of intellectual nourishment stand out. First, the rise of feminist historical scholarship, second the emergence of cultural studies, and third the shift in interest across the social sciences from production to consumption.

The new women's history that emerged from the late 1960s as part of a wider revitalization of feminist thought and campaigning did not initially display much interest in the history of dress. In Britain especially, issues to do with work, power and inequality predominated for feminist historians whose roots were mainly in social history. But interest in the experience of women in the past soon spawned interest in women's identities and the ways those identities were constructed and represented in art and the mass media. Dress is, of course, one of the key mechanisms of gender differentiation. It is also a key site of female expertise. Its study therefore acquired a new significance and respectability. This is not to say that feminist historians have always been successful at incorporating the study of dress into their work. A willingness to do so has often been compromised by an unfamiliarity with the subject and its technical difficulties.[2] Much of the best work on dress by feminist historians has been done at by scholars working in film history, design history and art history.[3]

The relationship of cultural studies to the history of dress is dealt with very thoroughly by Christopher Breward elsewhere in this volume. However, it is worth emphasizing here that, as with women's history, it was the growth of an interest in issues of identity, autonomy and resistance that increasingly drew the pioneers of cultural studies in the 1970s towards the study of dress. Early work in the field (by historians, sociologists and literary scholars alike) had bemoaned the vulnerability of working class culture to manipulation by the capitalist mass media. Such a perspective emphasized the heroic, political aspects of the culture of adult industrial male workers. It was suspicious of mass-produced fashions, whether in dress or leisure pursuits, and accorded them relatively little significance. But this was to ignore vast areas of the cultural experience of working-class men and women. Increasingly interest shifted to the ways mass-produced goods could be appropriated and used by working-class consumers to contest established authority. This development was most marked in the study of working-class youth subcultures that became prominent in this field in the 1980s. Given how important the self-conscious manipulation of dress is to the ways these subcultures so often construct their identities, it is not surprising that dress and its history began to receive more serious attention by scholars in this field.

The shift in interest since the 1970s across the social sciences from production to consumption has been the third important intellectual influence on the new academic interest in the history of dress.[4] In historical scholarship this has involved two linked developments, both of which have been beneficial to the history of dress: on the one hand, a loss of faith in that kind of economic history that privileged production in general, and the Industrial Revolution and the rise of mass production in particular; on the other, a growth of interest in the goods people acquired and the meanings they invested in those goods. As is so often the case in historical scholarship, these intellectual developments have been influenced by important changes in the modern world—in particular, the intensification and expansion of consumption since the Second World War and the rise of flexible production systems in manufacturing, most notably in the immensely successful Japanese export industries of electrical consumer goods and automobiles.

The history of the clothing trades always had an ambiguous relationship to histories of mass production. Despite the progressive expansion of ready-made clothes production from the seventeenth–century onwards, short production runs and rapid, fashion-driven changes in specification have remained characteristic of the manufacture of a large proportion of clothes. Clothing, therefore, never fitted easily into those narratives of economic history whose culmination was Fordist mass production. Since the 1970s, however, Fordist narratives have been challenged by a new emphasis on the continuing and indeed growing importance of flexible and artisanal forms of production.[5] From such a perspective the distinctive, fashion-driven features of the way clothes are made appear less a historical backwater than one of the main currents in the history of manufacturing.

The growth of interest in consumption has also moved dress towards the center of historians' concerns. Initially historical interest in consumption grew out of the search for a consumer and marketing revolution that reflected and might perhaps explain the classic Industrial Revolution.[6] Dress and fashion always featured very prominently in studies of this kind, not least because of the crucial importance of cotton clothing fabrics in early factory industrialization.[7] More recently, as faith in a single, all-transforming Industrial Revolution has waned, the importance accorded to the history of consumption has if anything grown. With it has come an explosion of work on the history of that most personal and expressive form of consumption—dress. This new work now embraces a huge range of issues and periods, ranging across the experience of rich and poor, the opinions of consumers and critics, and the influence of advertising and the mass media, while offering explanations that draw on theoretical traditions from psychoanalysis to political economy.[8]

The rise of women's history, the emergence of cultural studies and the shift in intellectual interest from production to consumption have been distinct, albeit overlapping developments. Nevertheless, there is a pattern to what they share. They each embrace key aspects of what has been termed the postmodern turn in the human sciences—a downplaying of long historical trajectories and deep causes, a focus on surface phenomena and on diversity, a concern with the personal, with the subjective and with identity. These postmodern priorities have worked to move the history of dress from the wings to center stage. They render important the very characteristics of dress that previously made it intellectually suspect—its ephemerality, its superficiality, its variety.

Since the 1970s these developments have provided the history of dress with a new intellectual respectability. The subject is now much closer to the core of mainstream historical scholarship. But with this new-found respectability have come new obligations. In moving closer to the center of intellectual affairs in the humanities, greater intellectual demands have been made of the subject and its practitioners. In a very real sense the study of dress in the past has been forced to lose its innocence. No longer is it possible to sustain a history of dress that considers its principal tasks to be those of establishing the time line of high fashion, or the chronology of changes in the construction of clothing. Questions of meaning and interpretation now dominate the intellectual agenda. This has been particularly hard for those who work on dress in museums. Inevitably their first concern is with surviving objects. Their intellectual work grows out of the close empirical study of those objects—their form, their color, their ornament, their construction. Yet at the very moment when their subject, so long subordinated, begins to be taken seriously in the academic mainstream, the careful empirical work at which museum scholars have excelled is called into question by those trumpeting the superiority of theory, sometimes in a language so impenetrable that it seems designed to exclude all but a narrow band of cognoscenti.

Yet for all the excesses of some advocates of high theory, excesses that amount in some cases to a fetishization of theory rendering it virtually inaccessible, it should be remembered that without theories there can be no questions and no explanations. It is essential that we address conceptual issues if we are to be clear-minded about what the history of dress is. This is not simply a problem of methodology, of how we go about the history of dress through the study of, for example, dress construction, probate inventories, or fashion plates. Methodologies in this sense received a good deal of attention at the "Dress in History" conference, but much less consideration was devoted to the kinds of questions those methodologies might address. Yet it should be clear that the broader intellectual developments that have propelled the history of dress to its new respectability have brought with them new ways of conceptualizing that history. These can touch even those aspects of dress history usually considered strongholds of the empirical, object-based tradition. Take dress construction, for instance. Usually it is associated with the need to recreate historical dress for the stage, but it can bear on a range of theoretically-driven questions such as the capacity of tailoring to reconstruct the body according to prevailing fashionable silhouettes, or the adaptability of certain styles to serial production.

What is required here is a new self-consciousness about the range of issues that the history of dress now embraces. Dress history is now a point of intersection for scholars coming from a variety of disciplinary backgrounds. Indeed, this is precisely what underpins its new prominence, nay respectability. But this is a more demanding world than that in which establishing the fashion time line across the centuries was the primary and apparently self-evident objective. It requires from those who study the subject a commitment to a mode of enquiry combining elements of both conceptual and empirical work. It has been too easy in the past for those who study surviving dress (often in museums) to criticize others for their empirical ignorance, just as it has been too easy for scholars whose work is theoretically driven (often in universities) to dismiss empirical researchers as conceptually naïve. What is required is not a crude pooling of approaches. Specialization has considerable benefits in scholarly as in other matters. Rather we need a willingness to monitor and reflect on other approaches. In doing so it will be necessary to remember that understanding the mindset of academic disciplines other than one's own can be a challenging exercise in ethnography that often requires at least a temporary suspension of disbelief. Nevertheless the benefits are potentially enormous. In the last thirty years, history has become much more than simply establishing a single, accurate story line. To say this is not to suggest that the empirical precision that has characterized traditional dress history at its best should be abandoned, but simply to recognize and embrace the conceptual diversity of current historical scholarship. Acknowledgment of this diversity is the key to putting the study of dress back into history.

Notes

1. See for examples of work that was essentially ahistorical, P. H. Nystrom, *Economics of Fashion* (New York, 1928), or E. S. Bogardus, "Social Psychology of Fads," *Journal of Applied Psychology*, 8 (1924), 239–43. J. Flugel, *The Psychology of Clothes* (London, 1930).
2. For example, L. Davidoff and C. Hall in their *Family Fortunes. Men and Women of the English Middle Class, 1780–1850* (London, 1987), 410–415 make a serious, although not altogether successful, attempt to incorporate dress into their analysis.
3. See, for examples which originate in very different areas of historical scholarship, S. Alexander, "Becoming a Woman in London in the

1920s and 1930s," in D. Feldman and G. Stedman Jones (eds), *Metropolis London. Histories and Representations since 1800* (London, 1989) and P. Cook, *Fashioning the Nation. Costume and Identity in British Cinema* (London, 1996).

4. For a challenging review of these developments, see D. Miller (ed.), *Acknowledging Consumption* (London, 1995).

5. See, for a very influential example, C. Sabel and J. Zeitlin, "Historical Alternatives to Mass Production: Politics, Markets and Technology in Nineteenth-Century Industrialisation," *Past and Present*, 108 (1985), 133–76. For the application of this approach to the modern clothing industry see J. Zeitlin, "The Clothing Industry in Transition," *Textile History*, 19 (1988), 211–38.

6. N. McKendrick, "Josiah Wedgwood: An Eighteenth-Century Entrepreneur in Salesmanship and Marketing Techniques," *Economic History Review*, second series, 12 (1960), 408–433 and N. McKendrick, J. Brewer and J. H. Plumb, *The Birth of a Consumer Society* (London, 1982).

7. E. Jones, "The Fashion Manipulators: Consumer Tastes and British Industries, 1660–1800," in L.P. Cain and P.J. Uselding (eds), *Business Enterprise and Economic Change* (Ohio, 1973) and N. McKendrick, "The Commercialisation of Fashion," chapter 2 in McKendrick, Brewer and Plumb, *Birth of a Consumer Society*.

8. The single most important monographic study in this new vein is D. Roche, *The Culture of Clothing. Dress and Fashion in the "Ancien Regime"* (Cambridge, 1994).

Fashion Theory, Volume 2, Issue 4, pp.391–392
Reprints available directly from the Publishers.
Photocopying permitted by licence only.
© 1998 Berg. Printed in the United Kingdom.

Annual Index

Articles

Book Reviews

Exhibition Reviews

Notes for Contributors

Articles should be approximately 25 pages in length and *must* include a three-sentence biography of the author(s). Interviews should not exceed 15 pages and do not require an author biography. Film, exhibition and book reviews are normally 500 to 1,000 words in length. The Publishers will require a disk as well as a hard copy of any contributions (please mark clearly on the disk what word-processing program has been used).

Fashion Theory: The Journal of Dress, Body & Culture will produce one issue a year devoted to a single topic. Persons wishing to organize a topical issue are invited to submit a proposal which contains a hundred-word description of the topic together with a list of potential contributors and paper subjects. Proposals are accepted only after review by the journal editor and in-house editorial staff at Berg Publishers.

Manuscripts

Manuscripts should be submitted to: *Fashion Theory: The Journal of Dress, Body & Culture*. Manuscripts will be acknowledged by the editor and entered into the review process discussed below. Manuscripts without illustrations will not be returned unless the author provides a self-addressed stamped envelope. Submission of a manuscript to the journal will be taken to imply that it is not being considered elsewhere for publication, and that if accepted for publication, it will not be published elsewhere, in the same form, in any language, without the consent of the editor and publisher. It is a condition of acceptance by the editor of a manuscript for publication that the publishers automatically acquire the copyright of the published article throughout the world. *Fashion Theory: The Journal of Dress, Body & Culture* does not pay authors for their manuscripts nor does it provide retyping, drawing, or mounting of illustrations.

Style

U.S. spelling and mechanicals are to be used. Authors are advised to consult *The Chicago Manual of Style (14th Edition)* as a guideline for style. *Webster's Dictionary* is our arbiter of spelling. We encourage the use of major subheadings and, where appropriate, second-level subheadings. Manuscripts submitted for consideration as an article must contain: a title page with the full title of the article, the author(s) name and address, and a three-sentence biography for each author. Do not place the author's name on any other page of the manuscript.

Manuscript Preparation

Manuscripts must be typed double-spaced (including quotations, notes, and references cited), one side only, with at least one-inch margins on standard paper using a typeface no smaller than 12pts. The original manuscript and a copy of the text on disk *(please ensure it is clearly marked with the word-processing program that has been used) must* be submitted, along with black and white *original* photographs (to be returned). Authors should retain a copy for their records. Any necessary artwork *must* be submitted with the manuscript.

Footnotes

Footnotes appear as 'Notes' at the end of articles. Authors are advised to include footnote material in the text whenever possible. Notes are to be numbered consecutively throughout the paper and are to be typed double-spaced at the end of the text. (Do not use any footnoting or end-noting programs which your software may offer as this text becomes irretrievably lost at the typesetting stage.)

References

The list of references should be limited to, and inclusive of, those publications actually cited in the text. References are to be cited in the body of the text in parentheses with author's last name, the year of original publication, and page number—e.g., (Rouch 1958: 45). Titles and publication information appear as 'References' at the end of the article and should be listed alphabetically by author and chronologically for each author. Names of journals and publications should appear in full. Film and video information appears as 'Filmography'. References cited should be typed double-spaced on a separate page. *References not presented in the style required will be returned to the author for revision.*

Tables

All tabular material should be part of a separately numbered series of 'Tables'. Each table must be typed on a separate sheet and identified by a short descriptive title. Footnotes for tables appear at the bottom of the table. Marginal notations on manuscripts should indicate approximately where tables are to appear.

Figures

All illustrative material (drawings, maps, diagrams, and photographs) should be designated 'Figures'. They must be submitted in a form suitable for publication without redrawing. Drawings should be carefully done with black ink on either hard, white, smooth-surfaced board or good quality tracing paper. Ordinarily, computer-generated drawings are not of publishable quality. Photographs should be black and white glossy prints (the publishers will not accept color) and should be numbered on the back to key with captions. Whenever possible, photographs should be 8 x 10 inches. All figures should be numbered consecutively. All captions should be typed double-spaced on a separate page. Marginal notations on manuscripts should indicate approximately where figures are to appear. While the editors and publishers will use ordinary care in protecting all figures submitted, they cannot assume responsibility for their loss or damage. Authors are discouraged from submitting rare or non-replaceable materials. It is the author's responsibility to secure written copyright clearance on *all* photographs and drawings that are not in the public domain.

Criteria for Evaluation

Fashion Theory: The Journal of Dress, Body & Culture is a refereed journal. Manuscripts will be accepted only after review by both the editors and anonymous reviewers deemed competent to make professional judgments concerning the quality of the manuscript. Upon request, authors will receive reviewers' evaluations.

Reprints for Authors

Twenty-five reprints of authors' articles will be provided to the first named author free of charge. Additional reprints may be purchased upon request.